tile|style

creating beautiful kitchens,
baths & interiors with tile

Heather E. Adams

Earl G. Adams, Jr.

Stewart, Tabori & Chang
New York

Published in 2006 by
Stewart, Tabori & Chang
115 West 18th Street
New York, NY 10011
www.abramsbooks.com

Library of Congress Cataloging-in-Publication Data
Adams, Heather.
   Tile style : creating beautiful kitchens, baths, and interiors
with tile /
 by Heather and Earl G. Adams.
      p. cm.
   ISBN 1-58479-450-X
   1. Tile laying. 2. Tiles in interior decoration. 3. Tiles.
I. Adams,
 Earl G. II. Title.
 TH8531.A33 2006
 747'.9--dc22   2005013281

Graphic production by Jane Searle

The text of this book was composed in Weiss and News Gothic.

Printed in China

10 9 8 7 6 5 4 3 2 1

First Printing

Stewart, Tabori & Chang is a subsidiary of

LA MARTINIÈRE

Dedication

We would like to dedicate this book to our family and friends; to our two rapidly growing boys, Reese and Rion; to the newest addition to the family, our beautiful niece Hayden; and to all of those who helped make this book happen. Thank you.

Acknowledgments

First and foremost, we would like to thank Dale and Carla Steinbach of Natural Stone Design for their expertise and enormous assistance in creating this all-inclusive book on tile. Thank you, Nick and Jason Patrick of Patrick Tile, for allowing us to shadow you and photograph your wonderfully artistic tile-setting skills. Thanks to Renee Foret and Sam Lundy of Foret & Lundy Builders, for the opportunity to photograph one of your many spectacular homes that made it through Hurricane Ivan. Thank you to our agent Stephany Evans, our editors Marisa Bulzone and Jennifer Eiss, and our book designer Allyson McFarlane—we make a great team! Thank you, Molly and Justin Brown, Susan Niesciur, and Robert Flock, for the use of your "props." Thanks to my dear friend, artist Reese Foret Verschueren. Many thanks to the architects, builders, designers, and homeowners behind the stunning homes featured throughout

the pages of this book. And last but certainly not least, a special thank-you to the incredibly gifted photographers who captured these amazing spaces on film. Thank you all.

We must also extend our gratitude to the following companies and individuals for their help in gathering information, products, and photography for *Tile Style*. In no particular order, we would like to thank Kristina Hearne of Walker Zanger, Dacia Delgato of Ann Sacks, Ryan Ross of International Wholesale Tile, Ted Lowitz of Lowitz and Company, Steve Turner of Plasplugs, Echo Mackenzie of Edelman Leather, Dominic Crinson of Digitile Ltd.—UK, Hannah Robinson of Rupert Scott Ltd.—UK, Sabrina Velandry of Eric Roth Photography Studios, Sally Trout of Trout Studios, Natalie Surving of Surving Studios, Leigh O'Dell of Pratt & Larson, Erica Ramuzzi of Oceanside Glass Tile, Jackie Smith of Gooseneck Designs, Lisa Wilson of Sonoma Tile Makers, Cooper Smith of Dal Tile, Carlo Menichini of Terra Viva, Owen Gale of Mainstream Photography, Beate Chelette of Beateworks, Lisa Schwartz of Schlüter Systems, Deborah Richter of Kohler, Piera Marotto of Marmoleum, Paulo Nogueira of Wicanders Cork, Jennifer Biscoe of Globus Cork, and Stephen Rosenblatt of Sonoma Cast Stone.

table of | **contents**

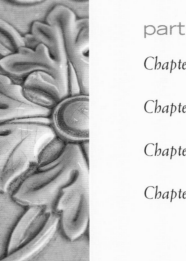

conclusion: Living with Tile

It is said that a picture is worth a thousand words, and in many ways, so is the face of a single tile. Antediluvian tiles in existence today function as pieces of living architecture, telling through their cracked and crazed surfaces the story of the artisans who dreamed them, shaped them, and set them into place. They speak of a time when talented hands were the craftsman's tool of choice, and the earth around him was his medium. These venerable tiles, delicately woven into the tapestry of time, allow us the rare opportunity to reach out and glide our fingertips across history itself. From the brilliantly glazed handcrafted bricks of ancient Egypt to the precision machine-made pavers of today, tile remains steadfast on its course into the future, maintaining its reputation as a material created to endure a lifetime.

For nearly seven thousand years, tile has graced facades and interiors ranging from the most modest dwellings to the grandest of public spaces. Remaining virtually unchanged in composition since its very inception, ceramic tile continues to be created from the earth's most basic elements— clay, water, air, and fire. Flash forward to the present, and we see Tuscan hillsides still dotted with family-owned factories that have been producing the world's most richly colored terra-cotta for centuries. Stone quarries operate to this day that once supplied Michelangelo with the pristine marble from which he carved his greatest works. Colorful glaze recipes concocted thousands of years ago remain shrouded in secrecy by the current generation that has been entrusted with them. It is amazing to consider that a building material that has

been in vogue for such an expansive period of time continues to grow in popularity at such an astounding pace. Is it any wonder tile tops the wish list of the twenty-first-century homeowner?

Once exclusive to the homes of the well-to-do, tile may now grace any part of the average residence with its luxury. Welcoming us inside are foyers dressed with spectacular inlaid tile "rugs" and intricate mosaic medallions. Monolithic floor tiles placed side by side entice us to journey further into the home as we follow their fluid path. Kitchens and baths continue to evolve and are now revered as monuments to the wonders that can be worked with tile. From the floor to the ceiling, this multi-faceted material steals the spotlight. Tile knows no boundaries; it invites us to escape the confines of the home, spilling out onto the veranda,

LEFT: Reclaimed French terra-cotta pavers set in a classic herringbone pattern support this home's authentic Mediterranean flavor.

TOP: Earthy, warm, and serene, this clean-lined bathing retreat features a floor of multicolored Brazilian slate.

climbing walls, and gracefully enveloping handsome outdoor features. Tile is everywhere, both indoors and out; there is no end in sight to its desire to overtake the home.

The ideal marriage of form and function, tile, in its simplest composition, is practical yet pleasing to the eye. Wielding great power and influence over a space, it possesses the ability to dictate a specific style or mood. Floors of rustic reclaimed terra-cotta or random patterned cobblestones that appear to have endured a thousand years of foot traffic exude Old World ambience. Multihued bricks zigzagging their way through a home instill the charm of an idyllic southern plantation manor. Smooth squares of limestone in colors of linen or mushroom form a quiet palette upon which to build a serene contemporary motif. No matter what style you choose to emulate, take comfort knowing that a tile is out there waiting to complete the look.

Making the decision to incorporate tile in your home is merely the beginning, as there are literally tens of thousands of options from which to chose. Categories include ceramic, porcelain, terra-cotta, stone, concrete, glass, metal, and mosaic. You can toss into the mix cork, leather, linoleum, vinyl, and rubber as well. Not only are there numerous genres from which to make your selection, but varying sizes, shapes, colors, textures, patterns, and finishes can be juxtaposed for even greater creative effects. Sizes range from the most minuscule mosaic chip all the way up to the massive three-foot square, with shapes running the gamut from the familiar to the unimaginable. Every color of the rainbow is represented on the market, with differing hues playing a vital role in the creation of dressy patterns, from classic checkerboards to trompe l'oeil tumbling blocks. If you stop to consider the abundant accessories and component pieces available, including borders, trims, accents, artist tiles, and one-of-a-kind custom pieces created just for you, it may set your head to spinning. Rest assured that with all of this assorted and ever-expanding material at your fingertips, tailoring an individual style that will elevate your home from mundane to fashionably chic will not be difficult. By blending tiles, inventively playing off one stunning material against the next, you can easily inject unmatched character and charm into your abode.

Within the pages of this book, you will discover the multifaceted uses of tile in the home interior. Our goal is to ignite your imagination, generating a firestorm of creativity within you. From hard-wearing floors of sleek porcelain pavers to towering shower walls clad in prehistoric stones, let *Tile Style* be your guide. Join us as we explore the variety of spaces that can be enhanced and transformed

through the addition of this versatile element.

Whether crisp, clean, and modern or dark, rugged, and aged, tile is one of our greatest assets in formulating a truly distinctive style. As you thumb through the pages ahead, you will not only garner many new ideas to expand upon but also become familiar with the tips, tricks, and tools that will allow you to tackle a tile project yourself. Step by step, we will lead you through installations in the kitchen, in the bath, and on the floor. Doing the job yourself not only saves you money but also ensures that your unique vision will come to fruition. When a little of your blood, sweat, and tears goes into the creation of your home, it is certain to become a part of you. Soon you will be taking that step back to admire your finished project. Take great pride in your accomplishment—you have earned it. Now, are you ready to embark on a new adventure? Grab your tools and ideas, and let's go.

ABOVE: Simple can be very pretty, as this kitchen proves. Cream-colored cabinets are treated to a rich chocolate brown granite countertop and subtle ivory-hued tumbled-stone splash.

OPPOSITE: Off white ceramic tiles capped with a substantial crown molding climb the walls in this romantic, feminine bath. The floors are the color of café latte, with tiny strips of mosaic crisscrossing each other within the grout joints. Complete with a chandelier, classic sconces, a soft cushioned bench, and a Calcutta marble countertop, this bath is the perfect escape for the woman of the house.

part I | **earth**

Chapter 1
Ceramic & Porcelain

Chapter 2
**Stone, Brick, Terra-cotta
& Saltillo**

Chapter 3
**Cork, Wood, Leather
& Linoleum**

When Earth Becomes Art

Molded from the very earth upon which we stand, tile is the embodiment of our past, reflecting within its mythical glaze the very essence of the culture that created it. Perfect and imperfect, delicate yet strong, ceramic tile not only possesses the ability to swathe a barren surface with exquisite radiance and vitality but carries a promise of endurance that can shrug off the passage of a hundred years or more. It is this combination of superior strength and irrefutable beauty that has given rise to man's love affair with this poetic material, and why it is found gracing structures in virtually every region of the world.

There is an ever-expanding list of reasons why we are drawn to tile as a home-building material. The most obvious, of course, is its good looks. There's no denying tile is beautiful and offers endless opportunities for creativity. But practical considerations contribute to its popularity as well. Tile is extremely durable and can withstand a lifetime of abuse if installed correctly. It is simple to maintain and easily repaired. Tile is a stable material that does not rot or fade. It contributes significantly to a healthy home, as its surface is hygienic, antistatic, and antiallergenic. Tile resists staining, repels water, and does not harbor bacteria or odors. It is relatively affordable and yet can add considerable value to a home. These desirable traits, among others, make tile a top pick for homeowners everywhere.

What is ceramic tile, and how is it made? Ceramic tile is simply malleable clay that has been baked at high temperatures to form a hard body. Raw clay is often blended with any number of additives, such as talc, shale, sand, quartz, mica, or feldspar, either to improve its overall strength or to reduce the likelihood of cracking and shrinking. Clay that has been formed, but not yet fired, is referred to as "greenware." Greenware is then placed inside a kiln, to be fired at temperatures ranging from 900 to 2,500 degrees Fahrenheit. Once the clay has been fired, it is referred to as bisque.

Ceramic tile is manufactured in several different ways, the most popular being the dust-press and extrusion processes. Clay used in the dust-press method is nearly dry when it is rammed under extreme pressure into steel molds or dies. The clay mixture is then fired under enormous heat, resulting in a very hard, precision-made tile. The extrusion process involves squeezing moist clay through a die or tube into a long ribbon. The clay is then cut to the desired size

TOP: White porcelain mosaic is bordered by a Greek key border in black. Lending to the classic mood of the bath is the tub deck, created from a marble slab.

LEFT: Subway brick tiles and marble mosaics pair perfectly in this stunning classic bath.

and shape before heading to the kiln. Tiles made in this fashion are somewhat irregular, with a more rounded body.

Once it has been fired, tile is either left as is, or sent back through for glazing. A tile that has been fired, glazed, and then fired again is referred to as

bicottura, or double-fired, tile. Bicottura tile normally features grooves, dots, or lugs on its back, which can make it slightly more difficult to install. In addition, it has a slightly softer body and a weaker glaze; the decorative possibilities it offers, however, are vast. Most household tiles today are monocottura, or single-fired. In this more up-to-date manufacturing method, the raw clay body and glaze are fired together in one pass, dramatically speeding up the process. Tile made this way is stronger, denser, and more cost-effective, but more limited in its decorative possibilities.

Types of ceramic tile

Unglazed tile. An unglazed tile is basically a fire-hardened clay slab. After one pass through the kiln, it has come to the end of its journey. Because this class of tile does not receive a surface coating of glaze, its color reflects its natural composition, and is the same from top to bottom. Examples of unglazed tile include quarry tile, encaustic tile, and terra-cotta. Shades run from ocher yellow to deep sienna brown; on occasion, however, the clay mixture can be tinted with mineral pigments, offering a wider range of color. Depending on the length and intensity of their kiln firing, unglazed tiles can vary considerably in strength and porosity. Because most unglazed tiles are either non-vitreous or semivitreous, they should be sealed.

Glazed tile. As the name suggests, glazed tile has received a topcoat sometime during the firing process. This glaze is a tinted liquid glass that is either brushed, sprayed, or poured on the face of the tile, and eventually becomes fused with the clay body through tremendous heat. Available in an endless array of colors, glaze keeps its final shade secret until it has encountered the searing heat of the flame. Many of the recipes for tile glazes have remained much the same for many thousands of years. Powdered minerals such as

iron (for red), cobalt (for blue), manganese (for purple), and copper (for green) are blended with silica and then undergo a heat-induced chemical reaction that results in the glaze's final coloration. In addition to giving tile the vibrant color spectrum we have become familiar with, glaze further alters its look through distinctive textures and finishes. Some tiles appear glossy, some satin, and some matte. There are glazes that produce metallic, iridescent, or multicolored effects, as well

RIGHT: A "wavy" countertop of glossy blue tile makes a bold statement in this modern dwelling. Malleable metal banding forms the counter's front edge.

OPPOSITE: Iridescent cobalt blue tiles with an undulating texture set the tone for the entire kitchen.

as crinkled, cracked, and crazed. As a glaze itself can be either very hard and durable or soft and easily marred, a scale has been adopted to help consumers choose wisely (*see "Abrasion Resistance" page 23*). Some types of glaze can stand up to use on floors and countertops, while others should only be used on walls. The actual hardness of a glaze is determined by the overall temperature and time it experiences in the kiln—the higher the temperature and the longer the firing, the more robust the glaze. It is also important to know that dark reflective glazes are often softer than their light-colored matte finished counterparts.

Quarry tile. Machine-made by the extrusion process, quarry tile is a very rugged, earthy material. Its surface can be glazed, but it is most often left in its raw, unglazed form. This primarily red-colored clay tile frequently exhibits flashing—dark streaks or marks caused by the reaction of imbedded minerals with the heat of the flame. Due to the high temperature at which it is fired, quarry tile is categorized as either vitreous or semivitreous, and is very stable outdoors, standing up well to climates that experience freezing. Its surface resists staining, and it provides excellent traction when wet. Quarry tile comes in three-, six-, eight-, and twelve-inch squares, as well as three-by-six- and four-by-eight-inch rectangles, with a thickness between one-half and three-quarter inches. Although quarry tile is considered more resistant to staining than other unglazed tiles, it is prudent to protect it with a penetrating sealer.

Porcelain. Porcelain tile is currently enjoying a surge in popularity, due in part to its endlessly versatile and virtually indestructible nature. Manufactured by the dust-press method and fired

in kilns at temperatures exceeding 2,000 degrees Fahrenheit, porcelain is classified as either impervious or vitreous, and is therefore considered waterproof, frost-proof, and stain-resistant. Because it is created by the dust-press method, it can take on just about any shape and texture, easily mimicking the look of stone, metal, and even wood.

Porcelain has evolved from a very plain, industrial-looking tile into the belle of the ball. Some of the more popular styles on today's market imitate silky smooth marble, serene limestone, and rugged slate. Further enhancing the illusion, porcelain tiles are often made to vary in color and characteristics from tile to tile. They are manufactured in sizes up to twenty-four inches square, and are now offered in a finish called rectificado, or rectified, in which water-jet technology is used to slice tile edges, calibrating their size and flatness to perfection. Rectified porcelain can be installed like stone, with very tight grout joints (sometimes called credit card joints). All of this hard work to rival Mother Nature has made porcelain tile a convincing alternative to the real thing, at a surprisingly competitive cost.

Porcelain begins its journey as pure white clay, but it can be tinted just about any shade through the addition of colored pigments. It is classified as either through-body or surface-glazed. Through-body porcelain is the same color from top to bottom, which is beneficial if you happen to chip the tile's surface. Any porcelain without a protective surface glaze must be sealed to prevent staining, however. Surface-glazed porcelain tiles are only as strong as the glaze itself, adding some confusion to the selection process. Because the color does not go all the way through the tile, their scratch and wear resistance depends on the glaze, not on the porcelain body. In actuality, some of these glazed porcelains are rated for light residential traffic only. In yet another class of porcelain, the body is tinted

the same shade as the glaze, making the tile more hard-wearing.

When it comes to installing porcelain tile, do not be surprised to see labor quotes near those for installing natural stone. Porcelain is extremely hard and eats up diamond wet-saw blades quickly. In addition, butt-jointing rectified tile is tough work, especially when the substrate is not perfectly flat. Because porcelain is classified as impervious, tiles must be set with a latex-modified thinset mortar for best adhesion. In addition, it is important to remember that the grout you select will appear somewhat lighter in color, since excess moisture is not wicked from the grout, as it is with some slightly porous tiles.

Encaustic tile. Rooted in the dark and mysterious medieval era, Gothic encaustic tiles endow a dwelling with a distinct aura of age and intrigue. Originally created in monasteries by British monks, reddish brown encaustic tiles were commonplace in the cathedrals and abbeys of England in the thirteenth century. Popular motifs tended to be mythological or religious, and included griffins, clovers, double-headed eagles, lions, family crests, fleurs-de-lis, and heraldic symbols. Each installation was considered an exceptional work of art.

The term encaustic derives from the Greek word enkaustikos, "burned in." The term refers to a technique in which pigments are mixed with warm wax, resin, or turpentine and then bonded to the tile by heat. Semi-wet clay tiles were carved or stamped and then filled with a contrasting liquid clay called slip. When the tile was dry, the top was scraped to reveal the design and then covered with a glaze and fired. Because the tiles were inlaid, rather than surface decorated, the result was a

LEFT: Large porcelain tiles simulate limestone when installed with a tight grout joint.

long-lasting material. After going out of fashion for a time, encaustic tiles became popular once more in the Gothic Revival movement of the Victorian era. Newer looks were brighter and fresher, and included colorful repeating geometric patterns, which made for a very recognizable period look.

Glazed floor tiles. Glazed floor tiles (also called pavers) are commonly dust-pressed mono-cottura tiles with a red body and an attractive surface coating. Tiles are classified as either vitreous or semivitreous and rated for wear by the PEI scale (*see "Abrasion Resistance," pg 23*). Popular sizes include eight-, twelve-, thirteen-, and sixteen-inch squares, and thickness falls between three-eighths and three-quarters of an inch. Glazes range from glossy to matte and result in a variety of looks, including a convincing mimic of rough-textured stone. Floor tiles are thicker, denser, and heavier than wall tiles, however, many allow these tiles to climb the walls, featuring them on the kitchen backsplash and on shower walls.

Wall tiles. Wall tiles are lighter, thinner, and less durable than floor tiles. Colors, glazes, and styles are endlessly varied and often include coordinating trim pieces, such as chair rails, V-caps, and bullnose. Wall tiles have a nonvitreous dust-pressed white body, so they adhere effortlessly to vertical surfaces. Tiles are soft and can be easily cut with a snap cutter, making it easy to fit them around plumbing and fixtures. Common sizes include three-, four-and-a-quarter-, and six-inch squares, with thickness ranging from one-quarter to five-sixteenths of an inch. It is important to understand that, as with lumber, the size of these and many other tiles are "nominal," and vary in actual dimension from one manufacturer to the next.

Mosaic tile. Ceramic and porcelain tiles two inches square and smaller are commonly referred to as mosaic. Used on both floors and walls, these commonly pre-netted tiles are available in a range of

grouting a nightmare. Some professional tile setters have devised a way of back-buttering the mosaic sheets so that the setting material itself becomes the grout, lessening this problem. In this case, choose thinset in the color you would prefer the grout to be, whether that is white, gray, or a custom shade. It is also important to remember that floors and walls must be flat and true, as any unevenness will be magnified under these tiny tiles. To learn more on setting classic hexagonal mosaic tiles, *see chapter 10, "In the Bath."*

Ceramic Characteristics

Moisture resistance.

When a tile is fired at higher temperatures for longer periods of time, it becomes more dense and less affected by water. In contrast, tiles fired at lower temperatures for a shorter time are more porous. The following classifications help to define which tiles are most affected by moisture:

Nonvitreous tiles are considered very porous and can absorb 7 percent or more of their weight in water. Unglazed, low-fired earthenware tiles, Saltillo tiles, and terra-cotta tiles fall into this category, and can stain if not sealed. Avoid using these tiles outdoors in areas that are prone to frost and freezing.

Semivitreous tiles are fired slightly longer and at higher temperatures than nonvitreous tiles and can absorb as much as 3 to 7 percent of their weight in water. They are best used indoors and should have

ABOVE: Handmade ceramic tiles form the backdrop to a floating slab of stone. The mosaic floor bordered with black mimics an area rug placed in front of the concrete bowl sink.

classic shapes, including squares, hexagons, octagons, pennies (circles), and chicklets (tiny offset bricks). Mosaics can cover an entire surface, or be used simply as decorative accents among larger tiles.

During the installation of mosaic tile, care must be taken that the setting material does not squeeze up between the joints, making the eventual task of limited exposure to water. Semivitreous tiles are not recommended for use outdoors where frost and freezing occurs.

Vitreous tiles are high-fired multipurpose tiles that can be used both indoors and out. They can absorb 0.5 to 3 percent of their weight in water. Within the home, these tiles are well suited for both wet and dry locations, particularly the kitchen and bath.

Impervious tiles absorb less than 0.5 percent of their body weight in water. Fired at extremely high temperatures, these tiles are ideal for use in commercial settings where cleanliness is important, such as in hospitals and restaurants. Examples of impervious tile include porcelain and glass.

Abrasion resistance. The Porcelain Enamel Institute (PEI) rates glazed floor tiles for their wear resistance. These ratings, which fall between 1 and 5, are designed to help consumers choose the most appropriate tile for a specific application.

- Class 1 tiles are for use on walls only.
- Class 2 tiles are best used in a light residential setting, such as a powder bath or bedroom.
- Class 3 tiles can be used in all residential and light commercial areas.
- Class 4 tiles are suitable for medium commercial usage.
- Class 5 tiles are manufactured for heavy-traffic commercial applications.

Caring for your ceramic tile

Caring for ceramic and porcelain tile is not difficult. Routine cleaning should involve removing dust, dirt, and debris by sweeping or vacuuming. Mop with a neutral-pH cleaner made for ceramic tile, as needed. If necessary, use a scrub pad to remove tough grime. Spot-clean as needed and attend to spills as they happen. Seal grout well for a lifetime of beauty.

ABOVE: Wooden strips criss-cross between grids of rustic-looking porcelain tile for a rich European look.

chapter 2 | stone, brick, terra-cotta & saltillo

Stone

Formed by nature and enhanced by man, natural stone is a building material unlike any other. Rich in color, diverse in texture, and virtually indestructible, it is the perfect addition to the home, whether featured in the kitchen, in the bath, or on the floor.

Through creative ingenuity, craftsmen pull rough blocks of stone from the earth and parlay them into a hundred unique variations, from the tiniest rippling mosaics to the most massive streamlined slabs. We mix and match endless arrays of size, shape, shade, and surface finish to generate looks as individual as each piece of stone itself. This wonderful element allows us a freedom offered by few other home building materials—to be as creative and as diverse as we desire.

Spellbound at first sight, many fall in love with the idea of filling their home with this timeless material which truly grows more beautiful with age. As stone becomes increasingly more commonplace within the average residential interior, manufacturers are relentlessly searching for new products and ideas. A stunning, one-of-a-kind design in stone—once well out of reach for most homeowners—has now become an attainable goal. Today, natural stone is much more affordable, thanks to rapidly progressing advances in technology—improved methods of quarrying, extraction, and fabrication have all contributed to reducing the cost of natural stone products. Stone tiles and slabs can now be cut thinner, so they are easier to package, ship, and install, and are competitively priced with most man-made materials. A home

enveloped in luxurious stone is no longer a dream but a reality we can all enjoy.

Granite. Lifted from the earth in enormous blocks, granite is the oldest, strongest, and hardest stone available. Due to its combination of vigor and good looks, granite has become one of the most highly regarded natural materials for the home interior. Colors range from silvery white to coal black and nearly every shade in between. Within this generous color palette are numerous surface patterns, varying dramatically from the familiar tight-grained, speckled appearance to exotic swirls and curves. Granite tiles are manufactured in a range of sizes, most commonly six-, twelve-, sixteen-, eighteen-, and twenty-four-inch squares. When selecting tiles rather than slabs to cover countertop surfaces, consider using the larger formats to minimize grout joints and achieve a more solid appearance. Surface finishes of granite tile are currently limited to polished, honed, and flamed and each finish imparts its own distinct look and feel. Polished

LEFT: A stove and vent hood combination creates a natural focal point in a kitchen. Spaces such as this beg for an eye-catching backsplash. Here, golden tumbled marble and handcrafted talisman tiles by Lowitz and Company form a beautiful picture-frame design.

TOP: Rustic ivory-colored travertine forms a stark contrast to the deep chocolate color of the Emperador Brown marble resting on the vanity.

stone is frequently perceived as formal, in contrast to the honed, which is viewed as more casual. Flamed granite offers a modern, industrial look.

Granite's large internal pore structure makes it susceptible to staining, so many fabricators and installers choose to seal it with a penetrating sealer.

In contrast, some fabricator's choose not to seal granite at all, allowing the stone to breathe and rid itself of any stains naturally over time through evaporation. If you are concerned with maintenance issues, request a sealer that offers a lifetime guarantee and rarely requires reapplication. Should you, at some point, have to seal your granite your-self, take care in knowing that it is an affordable process, and is as easy as spraying the sealer on and then wiping it back off.

Marble. Marble is an elegant stone with a rich history. Its smooth, reflective surface has been found gracing architectural monuments dating as far back as Greco-Roman times and its soft, luxurious texture has made it the medium of choice for many of the world's most renowned artisans. Once a luxury reserved for use in the grandest of public spaces, marble is now a prominent feature in the average home and continues to inspire greatness today.

Easily recognizable due in part to its unique spiderweb veining and glossy surface, marble is a decorative stone that commands attention. Colors range from earthy naturals to emerald greens, chocolate browns, and ruby reds. When these opulent shades are intertwined in delicate patterns, carpetlike inlaid designs, and grand medallions, marble becomes even more striking. Available in sizes ranging from mosaic to twenty-four-inch squares, marble tile is most commonly found in polished and honed surface finishes, but aged and rusticated looks are popular as well.

Despite its classic beauty, marble can cause dismay if you're set on maintaining its pristine polish, so become familiar with its weaknesses before deciding if it is the best material for you. Since its porosity makes it vulnerable to staining, marble requires kid gloves to preserve its original flawless finish. Sealing will help to repel most liquids; one encounter with an acidic substance, however, will etch even a sealed surface, producing a glaring dull spot. In most cases, you will need to consult a professional to restore the original finish. If you love the look of marble but are concerned with etching, it is wise to choose a honed or aged finish.

Travertine. Romantic and intriguing, travertine instills an instant aura of history within a home. Of all the stone types, it boasts the widest range of size and finish in the tile format. Travertine's color palette is confined to subtle earth tones, from the palest ivory down through rich shades of ocher, sienna, and rust. Its most striking color trait, however, is that it never actually appears as one solid color. It is only after laying out a sizable expanse of tile that you begin to appreciate its overall shading.

Travertine tiles are available in a wide variety of surface finishes, including saw-cut, honed, polished, tumbled, acid-washed, brushed, wavy, and bush-hammered. Edge profiles include chiseled, beveled, and pillowed. Ideal for use on floors, countertops, or walls, travertine only improves with age and wear. This beautiful material will require a little extra care, however, when selected for applications other than on the floor or in the bath. As a countertop material, it has several important drawbacks. First, travertine has a tendency toward etching and staining. A good impregnating sealer will provide protection from staining, but contact with an acid, such as ketchup, lemon juice, or cola, will leave a dull etched area on the tile's surface. Secondly, the chemical reaction between calcium found in the stone and acidic components within water can result in the appearance of water rings. And finally, the surface of travertine, in its basic form, exhibits tiny depressions and holes, a trait that may become bothersome in cooking zones. Several options are available to remedy this dilemma. One is selecting filled travertine, which is created when the factory uses a stone dust and resin combination

RIGHT: Cream-colored travertine and honed golden marble unite in this elegant bathing space. It does not take a great variety of materials to add interest to a space; simply contrasting color or running a border strip along a wall can make a bold statement.

mosaics to weighty two-foot-squares, it often costs less than many ceramics. Colors vary from muddy browns to intense shades of lilac, indigo, salmon, and sea green. India, Africa, China, and Brazil produce some of the world's most dramatic and vivid colors, whereas slate quarried in the United States tends to remain in the softer and more subtle shades of gray, green, and plum.

Slate is a very dense and strong material; acidic substances do not harm its surface, and once sealed, it remains virtually maintenance-free. While the process of sealing guarantees this care-free quality, it is prudent to experiment on a sample piece prior to treating the entire area. Penetrating sealers normally do not alter the look of the stone, so if it is your desire to enrich the surface color, it will be necessary to apply an additional sealer, or color enhancer. A color enhancer, available in matte, low sheen, and high gloss, will pull the deepest tones from within the stone, in essence creating a wet look. If you wish to maintain the stone's more natural appearance, however, be sure to choose a matte finish.

Ensure that you make the right selection by familiarizing yourself with the terminology that describes this stone:

Calibrated slate tile has been machine-ground on both sides, offering an exact, consistent thickness. Calibrated tile is much less labor-intensive to install than other slate tile.

Gauged slate tile has been machine-ground on

to fill open holes, resulting in a smooth and level surface. You may also opt to have your installer fill the holes with a matching grout or clear epoxy. It is important to note that in this case, slight depressions will remain. While the grout provided by your installer may be a better color match, the factory fill will be stronger and smoother.

Slate. Slate exudes a wonderful sense of warmth and texture that can be interpreted as rustic or modern depending on its neighboring design elements. Its unique undulating cleft surface stems from its composition of shale and clay as well as the splitting method by which it is quarried. Surprisingly, slate is one of the more affordable natural stones. In its tile format, which ranges from

ABOVE: A coffee bar sits upon a sea of slate, waiting to deal effectively with any acidic spills that may come its way.

RIGHT: Large twenty-four-inch squares of Chinese earth slate are given the freedom to move through the home and out onto the veranda. A home that connects with nature is easily achieved when the interior flooring is allowed to flow outside, uninterrupted in height and pattern.

one side, leaving the top side in its natural state. Though individual tiles may vary in thickness, they are kept within a predetermined range.

Guillotine-cut slate tile has a surface left natural on both sides, with edges cut by a chopping method. This process creates tiles with dramatically textured and rugged outer edges.

Random flagging is slate quarried in random shapes, varying significantly in both size and thickness.

Ungauged slate tile has been separated without strict regard to uniform thickness. Both sides of the tile are left in their natural cleft state. Ungauged slate can vary in thickness from three-eighths of an inch to nearly one inch, and requires an experienced stone tile setter to lay successfully.

Limestone. Velvety soft and smooth, with subtle surface variations, limestone conveys a feeling of serenity and calm. Often perceived as contemporary in mood, it is perfect for a Zenlike minimalist setting. Its surface is often studded with unique seashells and fossils, witnesses to its formation by sedimentary processes underground and in riverbeds. While its color range—predominantly milky whites, golden yellows, sandy beiges, and smoky blue-grays—is similar to that of travertine, limestone's surface usually lacks travertine's characteristic pits and depressions.

As with travertine, limestone's surface can etch and stain, so it is wise to seal it well and use extra caution when working with acidic substances. Some types of limestone are especially soft, and care must be taken not to nick their surface with sharp objects. On the other hand, there are limestones hailing from Jerusalem and France that are extremely dense and hard, rivaling granite in their sterling qualities of endurance.

LEFT: Neutral colored limestone tile provides the ideal backdrop to this home's rich wooden accents.

Size, Shape, Pattern, and Texture

Stone tile sizes range from tiny chips that can be scooped up by the handful to monstrous slabs you can barely get your arms around. The most common and readily available sizes include four-, six-, eight-, ten-, twelve-, sixteen-, eighteen-, and twenty-four-inch squares. Tiles vary from three-eighths of an inch to a full inch thick, the largest tiles being the thickest. While traditional shapes (square, rectangle, octagon, and triangle) continue to dominate the market, new alternatives such as diamonds and rhomboids are rapidly gaining in popularity. It is from these various shapes that numerous patterns and configurations can be formulated such as herringbone, staggered brick, octagon with dot, argyle, harlequin, pinwheel, tumbling block, and basket weave. For a one-of-a-kind look, consider mixing several sizes of one particular stone type, or mix a polished stone with its rugged, distressed counterpart—a subtle way of giving you a spectacular tone-on-tone design, in which texture and pattern variations become the focus of interest.

Edge profiles

When using stone tile for your countertop or vanity, you must take into consideration what material will best finish off the exposed underlying substrate (plywood and cement board). Options include the use of a matching piece of the countertop material itself or a cast or carved decorative stone border. In addition, you may consider a mosaic strip, a metal band, or wooden trim. When you design a countertop using tile, it is extremely important to determine the type of edge profile you wish to use ahead of time, and have it on the job site when installation commences. This is imperative, as the height of the substrate must be adjusted to accept the profile's specific width.

If you decide to install a honed material, such

RIGHT: Six-inch-square antique terra-cotta tiles form a simple yet visually exciting backsplash. Terra-cotta should be sealed with a penetrating sealer for ease of maintenance.

as travertine or limestone, as your countertop and wish it to resemble a stone slab, be sure to use the same material for the sink rail, and request that your installer round the edges using a special sanding technique. This process involves the use of an angle grinder, belt sander, or special wet saw profile blade and diamond abrasive hand-polishing pads. If you have chosen a polished tile, such as marble or granite, it will be difficult to match the factory polished look on the edges. Many seasoned installers will have the equipment necessary to round and polish the edge to a brilliant shine, but if this equipment is not available, the most affordable solution will be to cover chalky edges with a strong color enhancer. Once the enhancer has been applied, the stone's edge

will shine and blend wonderfully with its polished surface. New to the market are granite tiles that come from the factory with a thick laminated bullnose, eliminating the problem of how to cap unfinished edges. *See chapter 9, "In the Kitchen,"* for further information on how to use this bullnose tile.

Style

Each stone type brings its own unique personality and style to a space; therefore, it is vital to understand the characteristics indigenous to the material you are considering prior to making your final selection. On the floor, travertine and limestone provide a subtle and serene backdrop for those wishing to highlight more prominent elements within a space. Limestone, with its buttery soft surface, remains the number-one choice for creating a quiet contemporary appearance. Travertine, which has a bit more depth and character to its color, veining, and texture, is an ideal foundation upon which to build a variety of Old World looks such as French country, English cottage, or Tuscan farmhouse. In the bath, both of these stones perform exceptionally well, particularly when selected to envelop the shower. Because these stone types are able to be layered, shaped and rounded over, wonderful details can be fashioned such as arched

recessed niches and bowed bench seats. Although limestone and travertine are beautiful alone, consider dressing up bathing spaces, such as tub surrounds and shower stalls, with substantial tile moldings, tiny mosaic borders and deep relief decorative accents for even more drama.

Slate is the quintessential choice for those striving to create a visually captivating floor. Colorful and rugged, its cleft surface invites you to kick off your shoes and experience its unique texture with your bare feet. Perfect in just about any location

within the home, slate adapts to a variety of styles, from cozy mountain retreat to modern urban loft. It is important to realize that its varied color palette and high-relief surface are best used where they are not in competition with rival elements such as richly patterned furniture, area rugs and drapery. If you love slate, but are concerned it may not blend with the decor in your primary living space, consider cladding an oversized walk-in shower with enormous two foot square tiles. Place a rain shower fixture overhead and you will have created the ultimate exotic getaway just down the hall.

If you adore classic, formal, or elegant interiors, look no further than marble. From the stylish sophistication of black-and-white checkerboard to the timeless appeal of white and gray-veined Carrara, marble desires to make its presence known. When considering marble as your

LEFT: Antiquated stone tile creates a neutral palatte from which the rest of this bathroom's design springs.

flooring material, remember that its characteristic heavily veined surface can easily overpower a space. To make the most of its beauty, you may want to limit its use to locations where it can shine without competing elements. It is important to remember that polished stone has a tendency to become extremely slippery when wet, and softer stones, such as marble, will bear the scars of use in high-traffic locations. For improved durability, consider a honed or brushed finish, which will add traction as well as easing the burden of maintenance. If your heart is set on a high-polish shine in a heavy-traffic area, you may want to consider granite tile. In the shower, marble can be quite a head turner, but it's high polish will be difficult to maintain. Acids present in soap and shampoo will eventually etch its reflective surface. If you desire the dressy look of marble in the shower but do not want to contend with ongoing maintenance, be sure to choose the honed finish, or, once again, consider using granite instead.

Antiquated stone. One of the most practical stone choices, especially for flooring, is antiquated stone. Because its beauty lies in the fact that it has already been worn, battered, and roughed up, there really isn't much that you can do to destroy its charm. Aged stone is a master of camouflage when it comes to hiding dirt, and its distressed appearance is ideal for authentic Old World and Mediterranean interiors. Available in a

plethora of finishes, antiquated stone comes in tumbled, chiseled, pillowed, brushed, wavy, undulated, acid-washed, sand-blasted, bush-hammered, and random patterns. Following are a few of the aged finishes available:

Tumbled finishes are achieved by placing limestone, travertine, slate, or marble in a special tumbling drum, along with aggregates, chemicals,

OPPOSITE: Set in a random Old World pattern, cobble-edged travertine in a light walnut color graces this bath's floor. The staggered shower walls are comprised of the same stone in an eight-by-sixteen-inch size. Pebble mosaics, as attractive as they are slip-resistant, are the perfect material for the shower floor.

RIGHT: A Random stone fireplace is accentuated by tiny pebbles delicately placed within the surrounding grout joints.

or pebbles. This process creates a wonderful worn, weathered effect by battering the face of the tile as well as rounding and softening its edges. The technique was initially limited to smaller-scale tiles, less than four inches square, but tumbled stones up to sixteen inches square are now readily available. When installing a tumbled-stone floor, you may want to add a color-enhancing sealer or topcoat to draw out the deeper tones and veining concealed beneath the surface. Just be certain to practice on a sample tile first, as each sealer and stone combination results in a different effect.

Chiseled edges are normally found on aged marble, travertine, and limestone. A chain breaker or special drill bit is used to give the edge of the tile a highly distressed appearance, while the surface remains honed and smooth. This finish is readily available in square-format tiles as well as random patterns and sizes.

Pillowed tiles, as the name implies, feature a rounded tile edge that gives them a cushioned or "pillowed" appearance. The effect can be subtle, with a modest radius curve, or dramatic, featuring a deep radius depression. To maintain the pillowed look, make sure that your tile setter recesses the grout between each tile.

Brushed stone tiles are created when coarse wire rotary brushes are passed over the face of the stone, resulting in a worn, satin smooth finish, suggestive of aged leather. This finish begs to be touched.

Wavy tiles' undulating finish re-creates the look of tile that has survived extreme elemental exposure and endured a thousand years of foot traffic.

Bush-hammered tiles are battered by a machine that leaves behind a rough, dimpled surface.

Reclaimed stone flooring has been carefully removed from the existing homes, streets, and shops of Old World countries. These original tiles are unrivaled in their ability to add authenticity to a new home.

Acid-washed stone surfaces are treated with acidic substances that give the tile an aged texture and appearance.

Flamed tile features a rough surface texture achieved through exposure to extreme heat. This treatment, often used with granite and a select few limestones, causes the stone's surface to become dull and highly slip-resistant.

Care. One of the major enemies of any flooring surface is abrasion, and stone is no exception. Wear most commonly occurs when foot traffic and dirt particles collide to create friction. Taking a few precautions to eliminate this friction will prevent the premature aging of your floor. Place effective floor mats outside the entrance of each door, and remember that several steps are needed to rid shoes of dirt particles, so consider a large mat at your main entry, as well as just inside the doorway. Next, get into the habit of dust-mopping routinely, preferably with an untreated dry dust mop. You can also simply vacuum your floors; just be certain that the vacuum you are using is in good repair and rolls freely across the floor so it is not inadvertently scratched. Clean your stone on a regular basis with a neutral-pH cleaner, ideally one made specifically for your stone type. These cleaners are readily available at most any home center. Steam vacuums are also an excellent way to deep-clean your honed (not polished) stone floors, leaving them looking new again.

All natural stone floors must be sealed with a penetrating sealer to prevent staining. Avoid the use of a topcoat sealer/color enhancer in high-traffic areas, as the surface will tend to scuff and scratch over time, and may have to be professionally refinished. Caring for a stone floor is easy if you educate yourself and choose a finish that will not be difficult to maintain.

Stone countertops should also be sealed with a penetrating sealer to lock out porosity and prevent staining. Understanding the qualities of the stone you choose will help determine the best maintenance routine. Marble, travertine and limestone will etch if allowed to come in contact with acids, however granite, soapstone and slate will not. All countertops take significant abuse and each material, whether natural or man made, has its drawbacks. Take a close look at your lifestyle and cooking routines to determine what material best suits you. As far as upkeep is concerned, a quick wipe down with a neutral pH cleaner or stone soap will keep your countertop looking its best. Be smart and employ preventative measures by using cutting boards and coasters routinely and wiping spills as they occur.

Caring for natural stone in the bath is similar to other areas of the home. Seal the stone well with a penetrating sealer, clean as needed with a neutral pH cleaner, and keep on top of dirt and debris. There are special antibacterial cleaners made specifically for use with natural stone in the bath and will not harm or etch its surface. If you know your stone and know how to care for it, it will reward you with a lifetime of beauty.

Brick

When you think of brick, what comes to mind? The floors of an old Chicago brownstone, the walls of a New York City loft apartment, a warm and inviting inglenook in an Arts and Crafts–style home, the loggia of a French colonial plantation house? Brick is one of the oldest and most widely used building materials in the world today. Its easily recognizable oblong shape is natural, robust, and nostalgic, and its enduring qualities make it ideal for a wide variety of applications. Small in stature but tough as nails, this nonfading and slip-resistant material laughs in the face of harsh chemicals and elemental exposure. If you are looking for a material that is as attractive as it is utilitarian, look no further than brick.

ABOVE: Reclaimed antique brick set in a basket weave pattern makes for visually stunning floor.

History. The first recorded use of brick dates back to the early cultures that populated the lands between the Tigris and Euphrates Rivers. Molded by hand and left to dry in the sun, primitive bricks were first fashioned in the ancient city of Mesopotamia (modern Iraq) for a variety of uses. As civilization spread east and west from the

Middle East, so did the use of this versatile material. The great wall of China was erected using both fired and sun-dried bricks, and the reconstruction of Rome's Parthenon featured their inclusion as well. Brick was used as an architectural medium more in early Europe than in any other area in the world, and was of particular importance in containing the fires that raged through medieval cities. In the Middle Ages, floors composed of brick laid on edge were considered an advance over floors of beaten earth, and served as a substitute for the heavier and more costly flagstone in rural and less well-to-do communities. Eventually making the journey across the Atlantic into the New World, brick was widely used in construction by early European settlers skilled in the craft. This durable classic is featured everywhere from residential to commercial structures and remains a pillar of the home-building industry today.

What is brick, and how is it made?

Brick is a rectangular block fashioned from a clay mixture and kiln-fired for strength, hardness, and heat resistance. Early brick makers made these units no larger than any one man could easily carry. Today brick is made in much the same way, but instead of being shaped by hand, it is machine-produced. First clay is dug, then mixed, formed, and allowed to dry. It is then fired, and allowed to cool.

Color, size, shape, texture, and pattern.

The colors of brick range the scale of earthy natural tones and include cream, taupe, blush pink, salmon, orange, rust, red, gray, and plum. Some pieces are solid in color, while others are mottled and tinged with black. Most bricks wear the color of the clay that was used to create them, but some also reflect the introduction of various colored pigments. In addition to the composition of the clay itself, manufacturing methods also contribute to the final color. Fireclays (clays containing the mineral kaolinite, plus impurities such as iron oxides) are associated with lighter colors; ordinary clay and shale produce the familiar red tones. Manipulating the oxidizing conditions in the kiln can bring out shades of brown, purple, and black. Metals can be mixed into the clay that later react with the kiln's heat, creating unique gradients in surface color, a reaction referred to as flashing. Flashing also can be brought about by extra smoke and/or additional heat. Like most products composed of natural elements, no two bricks will look exactly alike.

Bricks are fairly standard in size and shape, but do vary somewhat depending on their intended use and manufacturing specifications. Standard construction brick varies in size, but is approximately eight by four by two inches. Sliced bricks specified for floors or interior veneer are commonly eight by four by a half inch These thinner bricks are much easier to install and keep the final floor height lower making thresholds and transitions less of a problem.

The surface texture of brick ranges from very smooth to extremely rough and can be directly attributed to the manufacturing process. The soft-mud process offers the look of handmade or antique brick, while the dry-press method results in a smooth surface. The stiff-mud process offers the widest range of possibilities, due in part to the technique of extrusion; extruded clay renders an even texture, however, the surface, or die skin can be removed to allow for a wider range of looks.

Brick's simple geometric shape lends itself to a wide variety of patterns and creative designs. Some of the more common types include running bond, stack bond, herringbone, basket weave, and pinwheel.

OPPOSITE: Brick flooring blends wonderfully with other natural materials such as wood and stone.

Style. You can be sure that when brick is used inside the home, it will make a statement. It is inherently warm and full of character. Depending on the architectural style of the home, it can instill any number of looks. Brick can be used on the floor or projected onto the walls, and even the ceiling. It is the perfect material to frame the opening of a cozy fireplace or to create one-of-a-kind features such as a Chicago-style brick pizza oven. Specialty areas inside the home such as romantic wine rooms, casual wet bars, and quiet studies can benefit from this quintessential material as well. Architectural features such as towering barrel- or groin-vault ceilings, rustic clinker brick walls, and gently arched doorways can become focal points around which the entire home is built. Creatively mixing brick with other materials, such as aged stone or wood, opens the door to even more varied and unique looks. If you are living with older brick you feel needs a face-lift, consider painting or whitewashing it to bring it back to life.

Installation overview. When you choose to use brick as flooring, make sure that the subfloor is strong enough to bear its weight. Experiment with different layouts, patterns, and grout joint widths (the most common being three-eighths of an inch) to learn what looks best in your space. Bricks that have been sliced thin can be set like any other tile, using the thinset method. If your project requires numerous cuts, it is best to use a diamond-blade wet saw, which can be either purchased or rented. You can also use a masonry blade on a circular saw or angle grinder to make small cuts. Prior to installation, sort through all of the pallets or crates and blend the brick tiles as you proceed for a nice flowing application. Once they are installed, and

have been given ample time to set up, it is recommended that you seal the surface well. This initial coat of sealant, applied prior to grouting, will help immensely in cleanup efforts, making it much easier to remove grout haze. After you have grouted and the grout too has had time to cure, go back and seal the entire installation with several more coats. A nonyellowing polyurethane will give you a shiny finish; a matte water-based sealer results in a more natural look.

RIGHT: This stunning walk-in shower is created from tumbled marble blended with antique terra-cotta. Handmade talisman tiles trace the walls in delicate waves and spirals.

Care. Historically, linseed oil was used to protect brick, giving it a soft satin patina. Today, water based sealers are the norm. Once sealed, you can simply sweep or vacuum to remove dirt and mop as needed with a mild detergent.

Terra-cotta

Translate the Italian terra-cotta to English, and you arrive at this tile's most basic definition: "baked earth." A more precise translation, however, might be "fired clay." For thousands of years, terra-cotta has been handcrafted by gifted artisans in villages throughout France, Spain, Peru, Italy, and Portugal by combining local clay and water. Simple, honest, and charming, terra-cotta derives its appeal from its very lack of perfection. Defects, inconsistencies, and color variations only enhance its magnetic beauty. Within the home, terra-cotta instills a distinct sense of warmth and feeling of antiquity, helping to create spaces that feel as though they have been in existence for centuries.

History. Terra-cotta's rich and varied history reaches back to ancient times. Along the Nile River, fragments of terra-cotta pottery have been discovered that are believed to date back to 10,000 B.C. Classic Greek and Roman architecture employed terra-cotta for roofing tiles and primitive plumbing. Not long ago, life-size terra-cotta figures of Qin dynasty warriors and their horses were unearthed in China that may be over two thousand years old. Throughout the ancient world, terra-cotta has been used in a variety of applications, including building brick, roofing tiles, sarcophagi, architectural embellishments, statuary, and utilitarian objects such as jars, pitchers, and kitchenware. In households that were unable to afford more expensive natural stone, terra-cotta was finished and faux painted to resemble the high-end material of the day, such as polished marble or bronze. As time marches on, terra-cotta

TOP: Antique French terra-cotta weaves its way out of doors in a classic herringbone motif. Terra-cotta tiles like these are often reclaimed from old European dwellings and exported to the United States, while some companies specialize in accurately reproducing them.

has refused to relinquish its foothold; it remains at the forefront of design as the perfect medium for bringing timeworn allure to a home.

What is terra-cotta, and how is it made? Terra-cotta, in its raw form, is a composition of clay and water made either through machine extrusion or by hand. It is a low-fired material, therefore it is nonvitreous and porous in nature. Depending on its region of origin, terra-cotta displays a unique coloration given to it by the various shades of local clay. The kilns used to fire terra-cotta can be heated by modern means

such as electricity or gas, or fueled by more primitive materials—wood, coal, or even olive pits.

Color, size, shape, texture, and pattern. Terra-cotta reflects the color of the clay from which it is made, and each area of the world offers something a little different. Variations in shade also occur depending on the firing method employed. A tile made in Provence, for example, is often a characteristic rosy pink, whereas tiles from Bordeaux and Tuscany may be ocher yellow or buff in color. In Spain, rusty red is the norm, while in Mexico, tiles are an orange-red tinged with soft gold. Wood-fired terra-cotta displays a more dynamic range of color variations, whereas gas- or coal-fired tile is bit more solid and subdued. Some tiles exhibit flashing, with their faces stained with sooty black.

Common terra-cotta tile sizes include four- to sixteen-inch squares, as well as two-by-four-, three-by-six-, and six-by-twelve-inch rectangles, which are often at least a half inch thick. Shapes begin with these basics and then move into the more advanced forms of octagons, hexagons, diamonds, pickets, and Moorish ogees. Textures range from soft and smooth to sandy and rough, and surfaces may be wavy and irregular. Edges can be either square, rounded over, or quite possibly, curved upward. Rest assured, each tile will vary a little from the next.

Terra-cotta tiles can be set in a variety of patterns, from jack-on-jack grids and diagonals to elaborate running bonds and herringbones. Some creative ideas you might consider when working with terra-cotta include blending it with other materials—brilliant hand-painted tiles, aged

LEFT: Antique French parefeuille terra-cotta forms the stair treads, while earthy geometric glazed tiles line the risers of this lovely staircase.

RIGHT: Simple handcrafted squares of Saltillo tile make for a warm welcome in this quaint English cottage.

stones, or intersecting wooden pickets. Tiles can be dyed, stained, or whitewashed. They can also be placed upside down for a unique leathery appearance, and then waxed with a combination of boiled linseed oil and beeswax for a stunning patina.

Installation overview. Begin with a substrate that is flat, strong, and clean, ideally one comprised of concrete or cement board over plywood. When placing your tile order, be sure to include an extra 10 percent to cover any miscuts, waste, and breakage, and to keep a few pieces on hand for future repairs. Plan and graph your installation carefully, then measure and mark the center of the room. Check your room for square, then snap intersecting reference lines with chalk. To insure a pleasing layout, consider creating a complete grid system thoughout the room. Work in

small sections (or grids)—approximately four to six square feet at a time. Observe the tile backs for dust and debris and be sure that they are clean before setting. Install the tiles using gray modified thinset, and a large half-inch square-notched trowel. It is best to cut the tiles with a wet saw, but small cuts can be made with a circular saw or angle grinder fitted with a masonry blade. Back-butter tiles to ensure even coverage and level installation. Check for level frequently as you move along. Once the tiles are set and have had time to cure, seal them well before you move on to the next step of grouting. After the grout has cured, seal both tile and grout again, possibly twice more.

Care. Once it has been sealed, maintenance of terra-cotta is fairly straightforward. Stay on top of dirt by routinely sweeping and vacuuming. Damp-mop with a neutral-pH cleaner, preferably one made for terra-cotta. Periodically assess the surface to see if the sealer is holding up, or requires reapplication. *(See "Saltillo Tile," below, for more on sealing porous tile.)*

Saltillo

The recipe and manufacturing methods for Saltillo tile, brought to North America by the Spaniards hundreds of years ago, remains largely the same today. Northern Mexico, the region of the town of Saltillo, offers just the right blend of clay, climate, and dedicated workers to produce these handsome tiles. Their soft, multihued terra-cotta bodies have become tremendously popular in homes across the globe. One reason behind their broad appeal is the rare combination of handcrafted good looks and exceptional low cost (around $1 per square foot). Fairly easy to install and care for, Saltillos age well and acquire a lovely patina over time. Their variegated pastel colors lend themselves beautifully to a variety of styles, including English cottage, Mediterranean villa, and Spanish mission. Offering endless versatility, these earthy tiles provide an

organic connection with nature when allowed to flow unbroken from inside the house to the outdoors, though this is only possible in temperate climates. Considering these qualities, Saltillos make good sense, especially for those who desire a home filled with character and charm but are working within a limited budget.

What is Saltillo tile, and how is it made? Saltillo is a handmade tile formed from the regional clays of northern Mexico. Local craftsmen mine the earth from nearby pits and then hand-mold the moist clay. Once formed, the tiles are placed on wooden racks and left to dry in the sun. Some of these racks are located at ground level, within the reach of curious creatures; you can often find Saltillos bearing the imprint of the tracks of dogs, cats, deer, and roosters. Many people believe that Saltillos are exclusively sun-dried tiles, but this is not entirely true; sun-drying is in fact just one step in the manufacturing process. After this first drying, the tiles are low-fired in a "beehive" kiln. It is the way that these tiles are stacked and positioned within the kiln that produces their unique shading and range of color, from soft ocher yellow to an orangey red. The tiles set closest to the flame exhibit a more yellow coloration, while those farther from the fire appear more red. Stripes are visible on tiles that are overlapped when stacked inside the kiln. Once the firing process is completed, the result is a soft, porous, unglazed tile with personality.

Color, size, shape, texture and pattern. Saltillo tile colors are fairly consistent from one manufacturer to the next, as they are all made from clay unique to one specific region of the world. The most characteristic color is a peachy orange-red tinged with yellow. There are several sizes from which to choose, including four-by-four-, eight-by-eight-, twelve-by-twelve-, sixteen-by-sixteen-inch squares, and four-by-eight-inch rectangles. The common thickness of these tiles ranges from 3/4 to 1 inch.

Shapes vary from square and rectangle to hexagon, octagon, picket, and arabesque. Saltillos also come in regular and super format; a regular Saltillo features square edges and corners, which give it a more rustic look, whereas super Saltillo's smoother surface and rounded edges result in a softer, more uniform appearance. Surface textures of unfinished tiles are smooth and chalky, with occasional chips and pits.

TOP: Saltillo tiles are the perfect choice for a Tuscan-inspired dwelling set high in the hills of California wine country.

Once sealed, these tiles may feel cool and slick, depending on the sealer type you select. For a shiny wet look, choose a glossy topcoat, but matte will give the tile a more natural appearance.

Installation overview. As with any tile installation, you must be sure your substrate is strong, true, and ready to accept tile. Saltillos are thick and are best cut with a diamond-blade wet saw, but simple cuts can be made by scoring with a circular saw or angle grinder fitted with a masonry blade, then snapping the tile along the score line. The latter method can be very dusty, so be sure to wear a dust mask and eye protection. Carefully plan your layout by measuring, snapping chalk lines, and working within grids. Saltillo tiles are far from perfect, and most have a slightly cupped backside. To prevent future cracking, it is imperative to back-butter each tile for even mortar coverage and use a half-inch square-notched trowel. Once the tile is set and the mortar has been given time to cure, it is important to seal the tile. This should be done prior to grouting to ensure ease of cleanup. Due to Saltillos' thickness and the wider joints associated with them (anywhere from one-half inch to two inches), a large amount of grout will be required. Once the grout has had time to cure (normally forty-eight to seventy-two hours), the surface and grout should be sealed once or twice more.

Care. Not all that long ago, Saltillo and terra-cotta tiles were maintained by oiling and waxing. Today, however, most installations are sealed with a water-based penetrating sealer. To bring out deeper tones in the tile, you may want to apply a topcoat sealer or color enhancer. To keep the installation looking its best, simply sweep, vacuum, and damp-mop with a neutral-pH cleaner as needed. Test your floor routinely to evaluate its porosity and assess whether additional sealer needs to be reapplied. If you begin to notice that water is soaking in, rather than beading on top, it is time to reseal. The procedure is not difficult, but may be a little time-consuming if you need to rearrange furniture and reroute foot traffic for a day. Sealers are typically applied with either a sponge mop or a hand-held sprayer. A generous coat should be applied and given time to soak in. Any remaining sealer left on the surface should then be wiped away with a soft cloth. How often you need to reseal your Saltillo depends largely on the grade of the original product used as well as the amount of traffic and abuse the tile receives. Presealed Saltillo tile is also available, but carries a slightly higher price tag.

OPPOSITE: Terra-cotta tiles run down this hallway, periodically interrupted by strips of ivory-colored stone.

RIGHT: Terra-cotta floor tiles provide a warm foundation upon which to build a light and airy bath. Long curtains placed on a circular rod make a striking and unusual focal point.

chapter 3 | cork, wood, leather & linoleum

Cork

Cork is an all-natural building material that comes from a renewable source, the cork oak tree. The cork oak, Quercus suber, is the only tree on the planet whose bark can regenerate itself after harvest, over and over. The bark is peeled off by hand every nine years, on average; as these trees, native to the subtropical Mediterranean basin, live to the ripe old age of five to eight hundred years, it quickly becomes obvious why cork is considered so environmentally friendly. With over two hundred million closed air cells per cubic inch, cork boasts an incomparable resilience and comfort. Moisture resistant and unaffected by humidity, it is the perfect choice for bathrooms and basements. An excellent insulator, it also absorbs sound effectively. As if all this weren't enough, you can add anti-allergenic and anti-static qualities to cork's impressive list of credentials as well.

Style, shape, color, size, and pattern.
Cork is the chameleon of tiles, able to take on the look of a variety of high-end materials such as travertine, wood, and leather. As time goes by, it develops a lovely patina, furthering the deception. Cork is produced in both tile and plank format, with sizes including six-, nine-, twelve-, eighteen-, and twenty-four-inch squares, and planks with widths of six, nine, or twelve inches and lengths of twelve, eighteen, or twenty-four inches. Standard thickness is three-sixteenths of an inch. These varied sizes can be creatively set in numerous patterns, from standard grids and bordered diagonals to herringbones and chevrons. Surprisingly, this uniquely textured natural material accepts stain more readily than most wood and is available in more than forty different color variations, so it takes only a little ingenuity to fashion a one-of-a-kind cork floor design. Through the marriage of imagination and artistic interpretation, these colors can be used to create something as routine as a classic checkerboard or as surprising as a gingham check.

Installation overview. Cork tiles need to acclimate to their intended location for several days before they are installed. Ensure that the subfloor, either plywood or concrete, is flat, dry, and meticulously clean. Be sure to fill any gaps or joints in plywood substrates, and make certain that a concrete subfloor does not present a moisture problem. Because cork is a resilient material, it will magnify any bumps or irregularities present underneath its surface. Plan your layout by carefully measuring, marking the center point of the room, and snapping intersecting chalk lines. Using a paint tray and short-napped roller, apply the manufacturer's

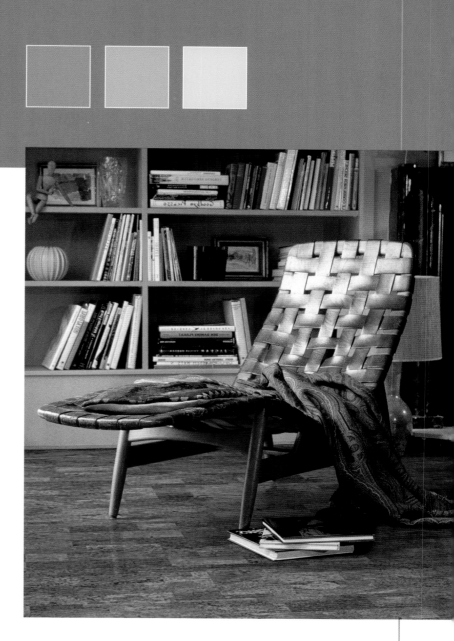

Cork set in a fun cream-and-gold checkerboard motif not only looks great and wears well, but allows the cook to stand for hours in cushioned comfort.

TOP: Available in strip and plank format, cork tiles can be installed to resemble a real wood floor.

recommended adhesive to the floor. Allow time for the glue to become tacky (about thirty minutes to an hour). As you move along your chalk lines, blend tiles from all boxes to ensure a nice color flow. Butt each successive tile to the next tightly, and run a heavy roller over them once they are set

in place, to ensure uniform contact. Make any required cuts with a utility knife. Most, but not all, cork tiles come with a polyurethane coating. If you're working with untreated tiles, you will need to follow the manufacturer's directions and apply the proper number of coats to your floor (normally

four). If your tile is presealed, all you will need to do is apply a final topcoat to seal the joints and create an impervious surface. Before you do this, be sure the tiles are clean, or dirt will become a permanent part of this topcoat. Use a foam roller to apply sealer, pulling it toward you to prevent air bubbles. Do not push the roller back and forth, but use single passes instead. Allow plenty of time for the topcoat to dry (normally a day) before walking on the floor. Over time, your cork floor will fade due to light exposure, something to keep in mind if you choose to use throw rugs over your tile.

Care. To ensure cork's beauty for a long time to come, it must be properly installed and coated with a water-based urethane. You may need to reseal your floor every ten years or so. To clean, simply sweep or vacuum as needed. Deeper cleaning should be done using water to which a small amount of wood cleaner has been added. Use a damp, not a wringing wet, mop. Avoid the use of oil or wax on urethane-coated cork. If refurbishing should be required, the floor may be sanded with medium-grit sandpaper, followed by the reapplication of one or two coats of surface sealer. With proper care, your cork floor will last as long as your home.

Wood

When someone mentions tile, wood is probably one of the last materials that comes to mind; wooden tiles do exist, however, and are very beautiful. At first you might assume this means parquet, but a variety of other wood tiles are available. Some are simply squares; others are formed from the end

blocks of lumber; yet others are a composition of smaller pieces that, placed together, create a wooden mosaic.

History. Originally, wood tiles were painstakingly handmade by craftsmen in Old World Europe. These delicate inlaid tiles were a sure sign of great wealth. Geometric parquet, made from oak, maple, birch, ash, poplar, and teak, was at the height of popularity during the seventeenth and eighteenth centuries, in styles ranging from Baroque, Regency, and Victorian to American Beaux Arts. As time passed, parquet became a mass-produced material, and the lower cost allowed these artistic tiles to grace the average home. In and out of vogue for years, parquet has surged in popularity in current times. Presently in

OPPOSITE: Blond wooden tiles appear as if they were ceramic with their clipped corners and dark accents. A durable finish of polyurethane is a must, particularly in a bathroom application.

RIGHT: Herringbone parquet drenched in a rich chocolate stain can be very visually exciting.

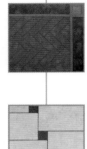

great demand are antique wood tiles and panels reclaimed from historic European châteaus and manor houses. The real thing may not be a luxury everyone can afford, so manufacturers have answered back with with authentic-looking reproductions that often fool even the most trained eye.

Style, shape, color, and finish. Wood tile is a warm and unique material capable of making a big statement. Of all the wood tiles currently on the market, perhaps the most well known is parquet. These particular tiles come ready to install from the factory and include numerous configurations such as finger block, crisscross, latticework, lozenge, star, floral, arabesque, cube, diamond, octagon, trompe l'oeil, sunburst, and basket weave. Elaborate geometric wooden parquet infuses any space with elegance, whereas the familiar patterns of herringbone and chevron impart the look of a chic Paris apartment or London town house. A variety of colors are possible, depending on the wood species and the stain chosen. For the most part, more popular tiles are oversize and medium to dark in color, versus those that are very light and small. Exotic beauties like wenge, afrormosia, and Brazilian cherry are beginning to show a strong presence in the marketplace as well. In addition to the color, finish goes a long way in determining the overall look of a wooden tile floor. For added drama choose a glossy top-coat. For a more relaxed and casual appeal, select a satin or matte finish.

Installation overview. Wooden tiles are commonly manufactured as tongue-and-groove components and installed by nailing and or gluing. Some tiles are available prefinished, while others require that you complete this process yourself. Before installing the tiles, check to see that they fit together snugly. Appropriate subfloors include plywood and well-cured concrete that does not present a moisture problem. Plan your layout, mark

guidelines with chalk, and prepare to set your tiles. After troweling on the adhesive, allow it to become slightly tacky. Place the first row of tile using the edge, not the tongue, to ensure accurate spacing. Set each successive tile by angling it into the groove and setting it down, then tapping into place with a hammer and wooden block. Make any required cuts using a jigsaw or circular saw. Be sure to leave an expansion joint around the perimeter of the room (about one-half inch) to prevent buckling.

Care. Wooden tile floors are cared for in much the same manner as any other wood floor. Minimize friction caused by dirt by using walk-off mats at entrances. Sweep, vacuum, or dust-mop daily. Periodically deep clean with a damp mop and wood cleaner and make certain that all remaining moisture is removed from the surface with a dry cloth.

Leather

Leather has been an integral part of our lives since early man first discovered that the animals providing him with food also offered skin and bones from which he could craft a myriad of useful products. Animal hides supplied our earliest ancestors with shoes, clothing, and shelter. They became goods for trade, canvases for artwork, and played a vital role in the creation of tools and weaponry. In medieval times, the Europeans understood the magnificent qualities of leather, using it to cover their floors and walls to alleviate the chill and deaden the sounds echoing through the cavernous castle halls. Once a basic life-giving element of nature, leather is now viewed much differently, as an extravagant luxury in our homes.

How is leather tile made? Full grain leather tiles are made using the process of vegetable tanning, the same method used for making soles of shoes and fine leather accessories. This tanning method adds life and longevity to the hide, making it extremely strong. Tiles are manufactured

from the strongest portion of the hide and sliced using steel dies and heavy-duty cutting equipment.

Style, shape, color, size, and texture.

Leather is an extremely sensual material, with its earthy organic aroma and silky smooth texture. Time is a friend, not a foe, as a rich patina develops over the years. Undulating colors of light and dark mingle with small wrinkles enticing our fingers and toes to caress its warm surface. Without a doubt, leather is the number-one material for

instilling unparalleled luxury in the home interior.

Leather flooring can evoke a number of different looks ranging from natural to contemporary. Perfect in spaces such as the home office, library, study, bedroom, home theater, wine room, or powder bath, leather tiles can be allowed to leave the confines of the floor and climb the walls to eventually cover the ceiling. This luxury item is not recommended for primary bathrooms or high-traffic areas such as kitchens however. Colors range

from pale blonds and auburn reds to raven blacks, and custom shades are available upon request. Shapes vary widely due to the ease of cutting and include squares (from four to eighteen inches), rectangles (including two-by-eight and four-by-eight inches), pickets, diamonds and random silhouettes. These varying shapes can be set in running bonds, herringbones, chevrons, basket weaves, and in creative trompe l'oeil designs. Textures may be silky smooth or slightly bumpy and rough with such unique options as custom embossing available; ideal for displaying a company logo, family crest, or one-of-a-kind motif.

Installation overview. Allow leather tiles to acclimate on the job site for a minimum of forty-eight to seventy-two hours. Be sure to blend material from all boxes to ensure an even color flow. Install tiles on a clean, flat floor, preferably one comprised of three-quarter inch plywood. Concrete subfloors must be dry; if they are not, a moisture barrier will be required. Next, plan your layout, measure and mark the center of the room, check for square and snap intersecting chalk lines. Working in grids, install tiles using the manufacturer-recommended adhesive. Once spread, allow the adhesive to become tacky over the course of about an hour. Set tiles in place carefully one tightly next to the other and press to ensure even coverage. Cuts can be made with a utility knife. Once in place, leather tiles will need to be treated with beeswax or carnauba wax, which will act as the grout and sealer. Apply two or three coats, buffing with a soft towel between each layer.

Care. Surprisingly little care is required for leather floors and walls. Simply sweep or dust as needed with a soft attachment. Periodically, you

OPPOSITE: Linoleum can be fun. Hundreds of colors and patterns abound, allowing for endless creative combinations.

may need to wax and buff your leather tiles to renew their luster. Spot-clean with a damp rag when required. Blot spills, do not wipe.

Linoleum

After taking a break from the spotlight, linoleum is back, and better than ever. Retaining all of its sterling qualities, this 141-year-old material now comes in a whole new range of fun colors and sizes. Reasonably priced, easy to install, and a breeze to care for, linoleum offers a lot of bang for your buck. Its surface is naturally antibiotic, anti-static, warm, quiet, resilient, and comfortable, and it becomes more attractive with age. Linoleum is also environmentally friendly, biodegradable, and does not emit harmful chemical vapors. Without question, it is a wonderful flooring material.

What is linoleum, and how is it made? Invented in 1863 by Englishman Frederick Walton, linoleum experienced its greatest popularity prior to the late nineteenth century, just before vinyl tile came on the scene. It is made from linseed oil, derived from flax; the word linoleum stems from the combination of the Latin words linum, "linseed," and oleum, "oil." The linseed oil is extracted from the flax and allowed to oxidize. Later, natural pine resin is added as a hardener, resulting in a linoleum "cement." Tossed into the mixture is a combination of powdered cork (which provides insulating qualities and flexibility), wood flour, and powdered limestone (which add hardness and strength). Soon thereafter, pigments are added for color. The raw material is then pressed into a woven jute or burlap backing and left for several weeks in a drying chamber, where it slowly bakes. Once cooled, it is ready to be cut.

Style, size, color, pattern and texture. Linoleum imparts a multitude of looks, from country chic to modern minimalism. Tile sizes range from twelve to eighteen inches square and feature

the surface of the tile. Linoleum can be damaged by moisture, so the substrate must remain dry. Allow at least two days for the tile to acclimate on the job-site prior to setting. As with all installations, plan your layout well. Measure and mark the room's center, check the room for square and snap intersecting chalk lines. Because linoleum is a natural product, be sure to blend tiles from all containers as you move along. Set each tile in place with adhesive that has been troweled on, and butt each tile to the next. Over the years, the tiles will expand to close up any space between them. Use a heavy roller over the tiles to ensure even adhesive coverage. Keep a damp rag on hand to remove any glue that may squeeze up between the joints. After installation, you may notice that the tile has a yellow tinge; this is common, and will disappear once the material is exposed to natural light.

numerous shades, from muted earth tones to zippy lime green, cobalt blue, fire engine red, and lemon yellow. Because linoleum's color and pattern extends all the way through the tile, from top to bottom, its surface hides wear nicely. Patterns and textures include wood grain, mottled, marbleized, polished, streaked, striated, or flecked; linoleum can be embossed with a raised design, or simply left smooth and flat. Perfect for anywhere in the home except for primary bathrooms, this durable material is ideal in spaces such as the kitchen, media room, mudroom, and children's playroom.

Installation overview. Linoleum can be installed over an intact resilient floor, plywood, or concrete. The substrate must be clean and free from imperfections, which will telegraph through

Care. Caring for linoleum is easy. Simply sweep or vacuum as needed. Mop with a damp (not wet) mop, using a mild cleaner. You may find it necessary to reapply the surface coating or wax in the tile's lifetime. Consult the manufacturer of your particular product for the correct procedure. Since linoleum actually becomes stronger over the years, as the linseed oil continues to mature, you can expect it to survive to a very ripe old age.

ABOVE: Linoleum once was the favored material for mimicking other types of flooring. Here, it fools the eye into seeing an encaustic tile floor from the Victorian era.

RIGHT: Large format linoleum tile is set in a subtle checkerboard pattern with contrasting accents at each intersection.

Chapter 6
Glass, Metal & Concrete

Chapter 7
Rubber, Laminate & Vinyl

chapter 4 | glass, metal & concrete

Glass

A fusion of bold color and contemporary style, glass is a fresh tile alternative rapidly gaining in popularity in homes across the globe. Perfect anywhere in and about the house, glass is both beautiful and strong, allowing for an endless variety of creative designs. Placed alone, small geometric squares march along to a modern beat. When glass tiles intermingle with rough and rugged stone, the look is irrefutably unique. Whether you use a handful of sparkling gems as accents or envelop an entire wall in a shimmering embrace, there is a style of glass tile for everyone.

Size, shape, and pattern. Glass tiles come in a wide range of looks; there are numerous sizes, shapes, and patterns from which to choose. One-, two-, four-, six-, eight-, and twelve-inch squares are common; rectangles are popular, as are triangles and diamonds. Escaping the confines of routine geometry, we find ourselves presented with a multitude of enticing patterns such as checkerboard, modular, herringbone, octagon, basket weave, latticework, pinwheel, and tiny offset bricks. In addition to these and other unique combinations, petite prepackaged squares in endless arrays of color and finish are readily available, just waiting to fall into the hands of an artist who can creatively weave them into an exquisite tapestry of glass.

Color and finish. Manufactured in a kaleidoscope of colors, glass tile can be translated into a wide variety of styles, tastes, and decors. There are literally hundreds of tones to tempt your palette, including sorbet hues of lemon, lime, and cherry. When your vision is of a serene spa-like retreat, soft blues and greens such as indigo, cerulean, sea foam, celadon, and sage will surely wash your cares away. In addition to being drenched with color, glass tile is also available in an assortment of finishes—translucent, opaque, and iridescent. Keep in mind that the finish affects the final coloration; clear glass appears rich and vibrant, while frosted glass offers a more soft and subdued look. Try mixing these opposing spectrums in the same shade to create endless tone-on-tone patterns and designs.

Glass style. There are numerous reasons why glass tile is perfect for today's home. Not only is it hypnotizing to look at and sensuous to touch, it is also extremely durable and environmentally friendly. Its sublime surface is vitreous, or nonporous, so it does not stain or absorb water. Glass withstands direct heat, chemical exposure, and does not fade. If its pleasing aesthetics and tough wear factor were not enough, glass is both versatile and dramatic. It is a mix master, blending easily with wood, concrete, stone, metal, and ceramics. It is ideal in all areas of the home,

Bright and colorful glass mosaics climb the wall behind a custom sunken tub of limestone. A glass "throw rug," complete with fringe, rests beside it.

from the kitchen and the bath to the floor, and can be used to jazz up a fireplace, a simple column, or even a plain wall.

Glass tile can be pricey, so if you yearn for its glitter but your budget prevents its use every-where, consider it as an accent in a field of less expensive tile. Choose to frame several square feet on your backsplash as a focal point, or insert a few tiny jewel-like pieces at eye level around your

shower walls. Place an inlaid rug design in your foyer, wrap a niche, or frame a door with ripples of shimmering color.

Glass tile's range of color, size, pattern, and finish is mind-boggling, with such diverse effects as netted glass pebbles that emulate river stones, or fragments that mimic jetsam just washed ashore, rounded by the relentless battering of the ocean's waves. Some glass tiles have a cracked and crazed

PROJECT

What you will need. *See "Tile Setting Tools," chapter 8, for a more detailed list of general tile-setting materials.*

- Glass tile—the amount your project requires, plus 10 percent extra for cuts, waste, or future repairs
- White thinset with liquid latex or an acrylic additive (avoid organic mastic, as it can yellow over time and does not bond as well)
- Three-sixteenths by a quarter-inch **V**-notched trowel
- High-quality diamond-blade wet saw
- Water swivel drill and small fractional core bit, if cutting holes in glass
- Hand-held glass mosaic tile nippers for custom cuts
- Hand-held diamond pad for smoothing rough edges
- Sanded grout for wider joints; nonsanded grout for narrow joints, or for tiles that easily scratch
- Grout-setting tools (grout float, buckets of water, sponges, cheesecloth, soft rags, utility knife)

Surface preparation. Glass tile can be installed on concrete that has had adequate time to cure (at least twenty-eight days), on cement backer board, and on drywall in dry vertical areas. Prepare the intended surface by cleaning it well. Depending on the location of your installation, a simple sweep of the broom followed by a pass with the vacuum will do the job. Use a wire or nylon brush to remove any stubborn dirt.

Planning your layout. Evaluate your space well. Take accurate measurements and transfer them to graph paper using a quarter-inch scale. Plan your layout so that equal cuts fall at the perimeter of your installation. Be sure that focal points feature full tiles. When working around smaller focal points such as plumbing, niches, and shelves, be sure tiles are symmetrical around each feature. It cannot be said enough—plan, plan, and plan some more. Dry-fit your tiles and work out solutions to problems before they occur. Once you have decided upon your layout, gather your materials. When tiling a wall, snap plumb and level chalk lines as you would when laying floor tile. Be sure the lines are perfectly square; if they are not, your installation will reflect this. As you move along, be sure to continue to check for plumb and level at frequent intervals.

Laying the tile

Step 1. After you have gathered all of your installation materials, the substrate has been prepared, and the glass tile has been delivered and inspected, it is time to get to work. Using the flat side of a three-sixteenths-by-quarter-inch **V**-notched trowel, apply a white thinset bond coat to the substrate receiving the glass tile. Work in small areas that you can easily work in twenty or thirty minutes, to prevent thinset from skinning over.

Step 2. Using the notched portion of the trowel and additional thinset material, comb horizontal grooves in the thinset, establishing the proper depth of the mortar setting bed.

Step 3. With the flat side of the trowel, flatten the notches to achieve a smooth, consistent setting bed approximately an eighth of an inch thick. Doing this allows for better tile bonding and prevents unsightly trowel marks from showing through clear glass tile.

Step 4. Apply the glass mosaic (paper side out or mesh side in, depending on the brand of glass you are using). Use light, even pressure to establish contact and avoid any air pockets.

Step 5. Use a beating block and hammer across the entire sheet to ensure adhesion. Be sure you have not used so much thinset that it squeezes up between the tiles. If this happens, start again, using less thinset.

Step 6. Apply each subsequent sheet so that the grout joints line up. Check that mortar is not starting to dry (skin over) as you go along, and continue to use a beating block on each tile.

Step 7. After fifteen to thirty minutes, lightly wet the paper face with a sponge several times over a five-to-ten-minute period.

Step 8. After the paper is sufficiently damp, peel it from the mosaic sheets, starting at the uppermost corner. Do this while the setting bed is still wet, so that adjustments in color or joint spacing can still be made. Readjust any obvious grout joints, so the installation appears as one solid sheet of glass mosaic.

Step 9. Allow the installation to cure for forty-eight hours before cleaning. Use a nylon brush and water to scrub away any residual glue or paper. Wipe clean with a damp sponge. Carefully use a utility knife to remove any setting material that has come up between tiles prior to grouting.

Step 10. Mix sanded grout in a bucket by hand with a margin trowel. Using a rubber grout float, force grout into joints at a forty-five degree angle until full. Remove extra grout by using the float at a ninety-degree angle.

Step 11. Allow grout to set up slightly (about twenty minutes), then wipe excess with cheesecloth. Because glass is nonporous, it does not wick moisture from the grout like other types of tile. The cheesecloth helps wick away some of this excess moisture.

Step 12. Go back over tile with a damp, not wet, sponge. Clean the sponge frequently to minimize haze. Perform the final polish by buffing with a soft, dry cloth. Be certain to clean tiles in a timely manner, or haze will be difficult to remove.

Step 13. Seal grout to prevent mold and mildew growth. Be sure to wipe or buff away any sealer from the face of the glass tile, to avoid leaving streaks.

LEFT: Glass tile projects a crisp clean image in this contemporary bath.

BELOW: Creativity is a wonderful thing, as witnessed in this stunning design. A damasklike pattern is created when a sandy-colored limestone is mixed with a slightly lighter shade, and a beautiful white bronze tile is placed at each junction.

body, while others are solid and uniform. Surfaces may be satin smooth or exhibit a textured relief—wavy, ribbed, or wrinkled. Tiles can be delicately handmade, with each piece slightly different in appearance, or uniform clones can be manufactured under precision factory-controlled settings. From appliqués in the shapes of turtles and fish to decorative trims resembling an opalescent string of pearls, there are no boundaries to the effects that can be created with glass tile.

Metal

Metal has existed since the dawn of time, and traces of it are in everything found on our planet. Its presence has been so vital to our history as a civilization that entire periods of time are

recognized by the popular metal of the day. The Copper Age, the Bronze Age, and the Iron Age are all ingrained in our memory from high school history class. Little could we know then that one day we would be running into the local tile store to peruse shelves lined with glowing metallic jewels, just begging to be woven into a fantastic

artists and manufacturers, metal tiles are now literally everywhere. Tiles created from bronze, copper, brass, zinc, aluminum, pewter, nickel, steel, silver, iron, and even gold can be found, in sizes from buttons less than one inch in diameter to the standard-issue four-, six-, eight-, and twelve-inch squares. Metal tiles come in just about any shape you can imagine, and are manufactured as decorative accents, trims, borders, field tiles, and mosaics. Surfaces might be shiny, smooth, and flat, or matte, rough, and wavy. From laser-etched and embossed to acid-washed and flame-finished, metal tile gives you plenty of options with which to generate a one-of-a-kind design.

Style. Depending on the style you want to achieve, metal tiles can be installed in mass, or scattered throughout a complementary field tile. Large expanses of metal can appear contemporary, cool, and sleek, while a few handcrafted pieces tossed across a powder bath floor can be subtle but stunning. An ideal companion to many materials, metal tile is particularly beautiful when paired with natural stone. Bronze, with its warm rich sepia tones, smolders next to pavers of craggy cobblestone, while silvery white bronze shimmers in a sea of colorful glass mosaic. Mixing all three elements—glass, metal, and stone—will surely result in a striking design.

design on our kitchen backsplash or interspersed among massive stone pavers on our floors. From daggers, swords, and armor to tiny decorative embossed accents, how the way we look at metal has changed!

Style, color, size, shape, texture, and finish. Once available only from a handful of

chapter 4 | glass, metal & concrete

When shopping for metal tile, be aware that there are varying degrees of quality. Some tiles are solid metal created at the hands of artists who spend years perfecting their designs. At the other end of the spectrum are ceramic or resin tile bodies that have simply received a coating of liquid metal. Distinguishing between the two is not difficult, as solid metal is heavy, and the color runs true from top to bottom. Look-alikes, on the other hand, are light in weight and show a different backside.

Solid metal tiles are ideal just about anywhere, but certain areas of the home—fireplaces, inlaid tile rugs, stair risers, vent hoods, backsplashes, and powder baths—practically beg for their inclusion. Solid metal tiles acquire a wonderful patina as they age. If you like, their original luster can be brought back through a little polishing, or you may choose to allow them to show their hard-earned character.

Installation overview. Setting metal tile is not difficult. Modified thinset mortar will offer the best bond, however, to improve adhesion, slightly roughen the back of a solid metal tile with sandpaper. Cuts are best made with an angle grinder or circular saw that has been fitted with a metal cutting blade, or a hacksaw for simple straight cuts. When grouting, tape off deep relief accents or borders to prevent grout from creeping into their recesses.

Care. Metal tiles are easy to maintain. Simply wash them down with a gentle tile cleanser and buff them with a soft rag to a brilliant shine. If you believe your solid metal tiles are in need of a luster boost, they can be polished up with either a pot-scrubbing pad or a metal cleaner. Do not try these cleaning methods with coated ceramic tiles, however, as they will scratch the finish.

Concrete

Not long ago, concrete was considered a functional, utilitarian, and "behind the scenes" material, essential for the foundation of our buildings but rarely

OPPOSITE: Antiquated stone mosaics pulled from the pages of history are peppered with beautiful falling bronze leaves.

ABOVE: Taupe-colored concrete envelops floors, walls, and ceiling in this surprisingly warm and inviting space.

found in the decorative layer. It is amazing how the ingenuity of man has changed our perspective on this familiar material. Concrete is still the super-strong substrate of yesterday, but now it has taken on new roles around the house in the form of countertops, sinks, vent hoods, backsplashes, tub surrounds, shower walls, and flooring. Gifted with the ability to disguise itself as other materials; at first glance, you might be fooled into thinking you are looking at natural stone or leather, not routine, everyday concrete.

How is concrete tile made? In simple terms, concrete tile is made from mortar rather than clay. The mortar is either extruded and cut from sheets or poured into forms. It can be tinted

lightly embossed with a barely-there impression. Concrete can also be waxed, buffed, and polished to take on the appearance of marble or suede leather, or treated with acids to render wildly varied streaks and pools of color. In addition, wet concrete can be studded with various materials, such as small pieces of stone or glass, to give it a confetti look. This quintessential material may be many things to many people, but at its most basic, it is a practical, organic, and sensual element ready and willing to accept its next challenge.

Installation overview. Concrete tile is installed like any other tile. Plan your layout well and make sure you have a strong, flat, and clean substrate. Make cuts using a diamond-blade wet saw and lay tiles using thinset mortar. Seal the tile's surface with a penetrating sealer prior to grouting and once or twice more after the grout has cured. Choose a matte sealer to maintain a natural look.

Care. Concrete tile is prone to staining, etching, and scratches; that said, however, it is otherwise virtually indestructible, and in time it will display a wonderful patina. Keep the tile well sealed with a penetrating sealer, and wipe up spills quickly. Avoid contact with acidic or oily substances, and clean with a neutral-pH cleaner.

many shades through the addition of varied pigments. Tiles are dried, not fired, so they are porous in nature.

Style, size, shape, texture, and finish.

Concrete can appear cool and chic or warm and bucolic. Large monochrome squares set next to one another evoke an atmosphere of tranquillity, while mottled tiles stamped with a random stone pattern imbue a sense of age. Concrete blends well with a variety of other materials, such as metal and glass, and is produced in a wide range of sizes, colors, shapes, patterns, and textures. You will find surfaces smooth as silk, grainy and rough, or

Vinyl

In price, ease of installation, and choice of color and pattern, vinyl is tough to beat. A synthetic material made from PVC (polyvinyl chloride), vinyl is a quiet, soft, and resilient flooring material that comes in both sheets and tiles. Tiles are waterproof, stain-resistant, and easy to maintain. More variance can be tolerated in the underlying substrate than for most other tiles, since it does not have to be unyielding, and placing them over an existing floor is acceptable. Repairs are simple, and removing a damaged tile for replacement is not an overly daunting task. Another plus is that a room can take on an entirely new look in a day's time. Tiles are easy to come by, with hundreds of colors and styles to choose from—so why wouldn't you consider vinyl?

There are two basic types of vinyl tile. The first, referred to as rotogravure, quite literally features a photographic image imbedded under a clear wear layer. In the other type, inlaid vinyl, the color is built up from the bottom. Inlaid vinyl has a more refined look, and because the wear layer extends through the entire tile, it is significantly more durable. With so many check marks in the positive column, there must be a few negatives to even out the balance, right? Vinyl tile does in fact have a drawback or two. Because it is synthetic and made from chemical components, it can off-gas, or release potentially harmful toxins into the air. It is also flammable and is not biodegradable, but it can be recycled. Vinyl's surface may be dented by high heels, and black-soled shoes may leave scuff marks on it, but again, this can be fairly easily repaired.

Style, color, size, texture and pattern.

Numerous styles can be created with vinyl tiles, whether glue-down or peel-and-stick. There are literally hundreds of colors and patterns from which to choose, and many manufacturers specialize in creating tiles that mimic other popular flooring materials, such as natural stone, metal, wood, linen, sisal, terra-cotta, brick, and ceramic. Tiles range in size from twelve to eighteen inches square and are available in several thicknesses (the best-wearing being an eighth of an inch thick). Surface textures include smooth, rippled, and embossed, with patterns varying widely from geometric to florals and everything in between. You can find tiles with photographic images of waves, sand, pebbles, and an assortment of whimsical themes printed on them. There are even vinyl tiles that glow in the dark!

Have fun with vinyl by mixing colors to invent one-of-a-kind patterns. Border the perimeter of the room in a contrasting shade, or create "tiled rugs"

or "runners." Or play it safe and stick to the classic motif of black-and-white check, as it never goes out of style. With so many options at hand, there is no excuse not to be creative.

Installation overview. The easiest vinyl tile to install is the peel-and-stick variety, as opposed to the glue-down. Peel-and-stick vinyl, however, has limited color and pattern options, and some tiles may be flimsy. For a long-lasting installation, choose thick, rigid tile, avoiding the thin and brittle types. Allow tiles to acclimate to the environment where they will be placed for about twenty-four

hours. You may install your tiles over an existing resilient floor that is flat and in good repair, but the best choice is to start fresh with a new layer of quarter-inch plywood. You can also tile over concrete, but it must be absolutely clean, dry, and free from defects. Before you begin, prepare your room, remove shoe molding, and ensure that whatever substrate you have chosen is clean, flat, and free of any raised areas that would telegraph through the tile's surface. Plan your layout carefully and test your design by dry-fitting the tiles. Measure to find the center of the room and snap intersecting chalk lines, making sure that they are square. Work in quadrants or grids, completing each one before you move to the next. As you lay the tile along your chalk lines, butt each one tightly against the next. Ensure that the first row is set perfectly straight, or it will throw off the whole installation. If you are working with a vinyl tile that exhibits unusual markings or a grain pattern, take into consideration how you would like the final design to look and lay the tiles accordingly. Tiles can be cut with a vinyl cutter, a utility knife, or in some special cases, heavy-duty scissors. As you complete each area, press down the tiles with a heavy roller to guarantee adequate adhesion. Once you have completed your work, inspect it well, looking for any problems or corners that may not have properly adhered.

Care. To care for your vinyl tile, sweep or vacuum routinely to remove dirt that may cause scratching. Avoid using a vacuum with a beater bar, as it can cause visible damage. Use walk-off mats at all entrances to cut back significantly on dirt that is initially tracked in; do not place rubber-backed rugs directly upon your vinyl, however, as

OPPOSITE: To play with scale and proportion, instead of setting a black-and-white pattern with single tiles, try groupings of four.

they can discolor the tile. Wash the floor with a no-rinse cleaner, avoiding anything abrasive or acidic. Employ floor protectors on furniture and take care moving objects—lift, don't scoot. Vinyl will scuff with certain shoes, particularly ones with black soles. To remove marks, use a damp rag dipped in baking soda. If the stain persists, blot with mineral spirits or rubbing alcohol. Vinyl tiles can yellow over time when placed in direct sunlight; keep this in mind when planning the location of your installation.

Rubber

Normally a material used in high-traffic commercial applications, rubber floor tiles are now making routine appearances in the residential environment. Rubber's nearly indestructible surface is endowed with enticing qualities—extraordinary warmth, cushion, and quietness underfoot as well as moisture, chemical, and burn resistance. It is a dimensionally stable product that resists scuffing and gouging and is flexible under heavy weight. Ideal in spaces around the house from the kitchen and bath to the mudroom, rubber tile can take significant abuse.

History. Around World War II, rubber tiles, manufactured from the milky sap of the rubber tree, were commonplace in homes across the United States. Tile sizes included six-, nine-, and twelve-inch squares in a handful of standard colors. As time passed, these sturdy tiles fell out of vogue in homes, and were no longer made from all-natural rubber, but from a synthetic mix of rubber, fillers, and resin. This super-tough man-made material then became the medium of choice for commercial installations in airports, train stations, gymnasiums, schools, office complexes, and retail stores.

Style, color, size, shape, texture, and finish. Rubber tiles can impart a very high-tech contemporary look to a home. Fueling this ultra-modern appeal are hundreds of brilliant colors, ranging from vivid primaries to soft pastels. A variety of sizes are available and include twelve-, eighteen-, twenty-four-, thirty-six-, and forty-eight-inch squares. Due to its commercial background, rubber is made to be safe, strong, and hide dirt. Its surface is often ornamented with raised designs such as dots, grids, diamonds, triangles, waves, circles, or may be embossed to mimic materials such as slate or leather. Flat rubber tiles are manufactured as well, but they may become slick when wet. More decorative and familiar surface patterns are marbleized, flecked, striated, and mottled. Both matte and high-gloss finishes are available.

Installation overview. Supple rubber floor tiles are easy to cut and lay. Because they are resilient, they require a perfectly flat, clean, and dry subfloor. Prior to laying the tiles, allow them to acclimate to the room where they will be placed for twenty-four hours. Plan your layout. Measure the room to find the center and snap intersecting chalk lines. This will separate your work zone into quadrants. Dry-fit tiles before setting them to ensure a pleasing layout. Begin your installation in the first quadrant by placing tiles along the intersection of your chalk lines, and complete one area before moving to the next. Set each tile tightly against the next. Rubber tiles are set with an epoxy adhesive, and it is important to follow the manufacturer's directions for the proper way to mix and apply the adhesive. Be sure to have a damp cloth on hand to quickly remove any adhesive that may squeeze up between the tiles. Once you have completed a section, press down the tiles with a heavy roller to ensure adequate adhesion. Depending on the brand of rubber tile, you may need to apply a sealer. Check with the manufacturer to be certain.

Care. Despite all its sterling qualities, rubber is still vulnerable to grease and oil stains, and may require resealing from time to time. Many industrial rubber products have a "self-polishing" feature, which actually allows the tile to heal its own abrasions. In a residential application, a general sweep here and there and routine vacuuming will be sufficient. Mop as needed with a neutral-pH cleaner.

RIGHT: This kitchen feels like a quaint French bistro, with its tiles of black and white.

part III | art

Chapter 6
Designing with Tile

Chapter 7
Artistic Tile Projects: Step-by-Step

chapter 6 | designing with tile

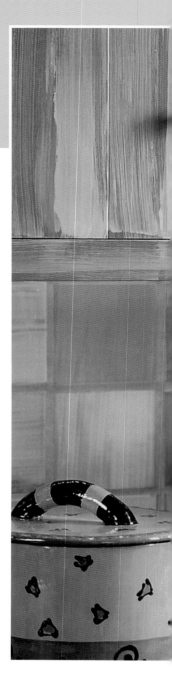

Designing with tile has never been easier, due in part to the fact that tile manufacturers are now producing clones of just about everything. Blurring the lines between what is real and what is not, the tile industry has reached the apex of success in the art of duplication, using advances in tile technology such as digital art transfers to produce tiles that look like original hand-painted designs, mimics of Mother Nature's most treasured gifts of wood and stone, and accurate re-creations of centuries-old terra-cotta. There are even oversize porcelain tiles that emulate fabric so persuasively, you might be convinced that your floors and walls need to be dry-cleaned rather than damp-mopped. To balance these technical coups within the ceramic industry, handcrafted tile is back, and stronger than ever, sporting hand-painted murals, deep relief accents, and delicately carved borders. New ideas continue to come to the forefront, and common everyday materials have found new life in spectacular tiles of metal, glass, and concrete. Add to all of this advances in production such as laser-guided water-jet cutting, and you have barely scratched the surface of the immense world of tile. With literally thousands upon thousands of options to choose from, finding the perfect tile will not be the problem. Surviving the selection process may be, however, so it is vital to enter the arena prepared.

The planning stage. To ensure a pleasing outcome, it is imperative to begin the design process by asking yourself several specific questions before rushing out the door to the nearest tile center. What is the main purpose of the room in which the tile will be used? What kind of foot traffic and or abuse must it endure? What is the general impression or style you wish to convey? What other objects will be placed in the space? Once you have a pretty good idea of the type of material you're going to use, activate your visual creativity by looking at books and magazines that feature attractive interior designs. Don't limit yourself to those that simply illustrate the material you plan to use; what you're seeking at this point is strictly conceptual ideas. Search for specific details in the way the material has been laid out and how that impacts the room's visual appeal to discover what speaks to you.

One of the great attributes of tile is that it can be used in every room of the house, from the entryway and living room to the kitchen and bath. Your primary concern as you narrow down your selection will be the wear factor. While all areas of the home can be tiled, it is important to understand that not all tile types can be used in all areas. Don't make the mistake of assuming that they are interchangeable. Floor tiles are very strong, designed specifically to take abuse

underfoot; while they may be used on wall applications as well, the reverse does not hold true. Wall tiles placed on the floor not only can be dangerously slippery, but simply will not hold up under long-term wear and tear. So before you rush out to find yourself overwhelmed by all the eye candy lining the tile showroom walls, research, research, research. Take a look at your project objectively before you leave the house. Have in mind a good idea of what type of tile you will be shopping for. Familiarize yourself with tile classifications with regard to water absorption and wear. This alone will help you to narrow down the selections, and prevent you from buying something that has more visual appeal than practical virtue.

Ultimately, the driving force behind your final choice will be your budget. Tile prices can vary dramatically, and are driven by any number of things,

not the least of which is overall appearance and durability. Another factor influencing cost within a specific line will be the number of accompanying trim pieces available. Specific tile lines that offer matching bullnose edging, listellos (tiles designed to be borders), and decos will definitely give you more design options, but typically carry a slightly higher price tag. A line that offers field tiles only may not be the best choice, especially if you're planning vertical applications such as shower walls, tub surrounds, or backsplashes. Don't fall into the trap of choosing an attractively priced field tile and then searching for Band-Aid solutions to cover its exposed edges, as this will inevitably lead to frustration and disappointment.

Shopping for tile. Once you arrive at the tile center, it is easy to become distracted, so stay the course. Take it all in, explore, but don't let yourself become overwhelmed. Keep in mind that certain tiles evoke specific styles; limit your preliminary selections to those that reflect the look of your home. This will not only save time but prevent the frustration associated with trying to force a square peg into a round hole. Remember, this often-pricey purchase will become a semi-permanent part of your home. Don't forget to bring along a notepad and jot down all the available information regarding size and trim options. Check that coordinating listellos and bullnose pieces are available if you are working on a vertical application. Even if you experience love at first sight, it is wise to take at least two other options home with you. This doesn't mean three wildly different tiles, but three that appear similar in texture and color, or at the very least a lighter and darker version of the tile you

OPPOSITE: Inspired by the mystery of Morocco, this intricate and colorful tile design begs you to leave behind your cares as you close the bathroom door behind you. Walls feature a glossy hand-made ceramic that blends beautifully with the antiquated stone floor below.

favor. The opportunity to compare them once you're back home will help fuel confidence in your final decision.

Reviewing choices. Once you're satisfied with your initial selections, it is time to head back to the house. Placing tiles in the exact location of their intended use will help immensely with the decision-making process. You will be amazed how your perception of a tile changes when it is out of the showroom and in a new environment. Your first assignment will be to reexamine the color. Many variables can influence the actual shade, such as the reflection of the paint from the surrounding walls or the glare from natural light spilling across the floor. Wood tones present in adjacent furniture and cabinetry can also cause you to view the color differently. Second, analyze the glaze. Is it what you expected? Higher-priced tiles tend to have a richer, more realistic surface finish. Tiles that mimic natural stone should have a matte glaze to enhance the illusion, unless you are choosing to emulate the look of polished marble. Remember, you will live with your choice for many years to come—so don't rush the selection process. It is not wise to make a snap decision on something this permanent. Play with the samples, mixing, matching, and discovering what size, shape, and color best suits your space. If you are working on a backsplash, lean the tiles against the wall and leave the room. Walk back in, and at a glance, you should be able to see if your choice harmonizes with the room. If you're seeking the perfect flooring, observe it at different times of the day. Does it ground the room and provide a solid backdrop from which your furniture placement can spring, or does it wash out in the bright light of day? Taking time to investigate, explore, and play with actual sample tile applications will further boost your confidence in the final selection.

Finalizing the order. Once you have decided on a specific style and feel confident that it will

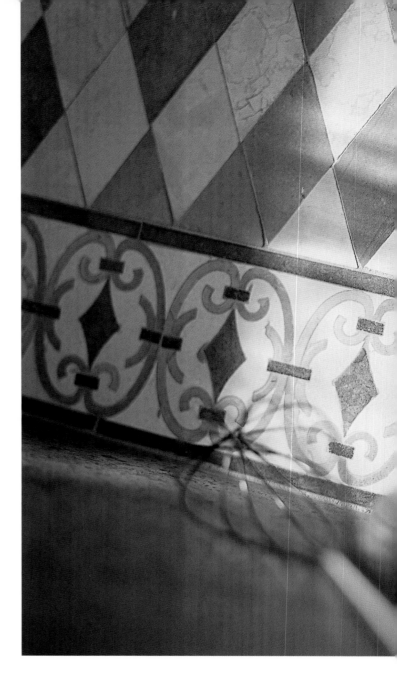

work well with your design scheme, begin making preparations to place your order. Before signing on the dotted line, you should be confident that you have asked the retailer all the right questions: Is the tile that I have chosen suitable for the area in which I plan to use it? Does it require any special care or routine maintenance? Is the material in stock? If not, what is the lead time? Is the sample I am ordering from the current stock, or has the dye lot changed? Would you suggest that I order a current sample or two if this one is outdated? What is your return policy? Be sure when placing your order that you purchase more square footage than you actually need (typically 7 to 10 percent more). This surplus will be your insurance against shortages that may occur due to breakage, mistakes, or waste due to cutting. Each individual tile line does not stay in production forever; at minimum, tiles will vary from lot to lot while actively on the market. A wise homeowner will order an extra box to ensure against future problems as chances of finding an exact match years down the line are very slim. Once your tile arrives, take the time to inspect it. As laborious as that might seem, it will save you heartache if you encounter a problem in the middle of the installation. Many freight carriers that deliver tile only give you a few days to make claims if the shipment is damaged, and the supplier typically will not accept returns once the shipment has arrived on-site and has been noted as safely delivered. In addition to checking for breakage, confirm that your tiles are the correct shade, from the same lot, and that your order is complete, with no missing tiles. Tiles do vary in color to some degree within the same dye lot, so it is important that your installer blend pieces from all of the boxes as he moves through the installation process.

Elements of Design

Color. If there is one single element that can instill a specific mood in a space, it is most definitely color. Color can make a very powerful statement, so the selection process must not be taken lightly. Take cues from your surroundings, such as your choice of artwork, furniture, clothing, paint, and so on, and you will probably have a good idea of what you are drawn to. You may be a lover of rich earthy naturals, you may prefer quiet neutrals, or maybe you're mad about bold, daring colors. Sticking with something you already feel comfortable with will be much safer than deciding to make a sudden and

ABOVE: The backsplash is the perfect place to add pattern and color in a kitchen. Here, earthy shades of limestone are arranged in a harlequin pattern. The precision-cut border blends all three colors for a striking motif.

drastic change, especially when it involves something as permanent as tile.

When choosing color, keep in mind that light colors recede, making a room appear larger, whereas dark colors advance, making a space seem smaller. In warm, sunny climates, light colors will evoke coolness, while going darker in colder areas will instill a feeling of warmth. Be careful not to lean too dramatically one way or another; too bright or too dark may not be ideal for your particular design.

Color can be quiet and serene, or loud and exciting. Hues can be combined to create unique patterns, or left solid to promote fluid movement. Color can also evoke emotion. White can feel cool and clean. Toss in a pinch of black, and you have a retro or ultramodern vibe. Soft shades such as celadon, cerulean, or lavender are soothing, while bright canary yellow, hot red, and tangerine orange can trigger heart-pumping exhilaration. Earthy organic tones of olive, linen, ocher, and rust impart a relaxed and laid-back mood. When you select the color of your tile, it is important to take note of the way surrounding elements will influence the effect. In a bathroom, for instance, take into consideration the colors of the vanity, fixtures, sink, faucet, tub, and toilet. In the living room, note the colors of accessories, drapery, area rugs, furniture, and cabinetry. Making sure your tile gets along well with its neighbors while allowing for change over the years will ensure a pleasing investment.

Size, shape, and pattern. Most tiles come in sizes ranging from tiny mosaics to huge two- and three-foot squares. The most commonly available sizes include four-, six-, eight-, twelve-, sixteen-, eighteen-, and twenty-four-inch squares. Thickness varies from one to three-quarter inches (though some stone and terra-cotta tiles are over an inch thick); as a general rule, as the size increases, so does the thickness. The most important aspect of tile size is its scale and proportion—its relationship to the space in which it exists. The goal is to be able to observe your selection in its intended placement and say to yourself, "Not too big, not too small . . . just right." Forget the "rules,"

as small spaces don't necessarily require small tiles, nor do large spaces require large tiles. The best size is determined by evaluating each room as a separate entity, and determining what size flatters it best.

Shapes range from the routine geometry of squares, rectangles, triangles, hexagons, and octagons to more exotic diamonds and rhomboids. By combining size and shape, you create pattern. Square tiles can be placed in a simple jack-on-jack

LEFT: Plain white tile can take on any number of looks. In this bath the colors and accesories chosen create a sweet feminine retreat.

RIGHT: Pretty and romantic, this bathroom's vintage turquoise and black tile combination is the ideal foundation upon which to build a shabby-chic motif.

grid or offset to create a running bond. Square tiles are also used for diagonal runs. Rectangles can be placed at angles to each other to form a herringbone pattern, or be offset like brick. Diamonds or rhomboids, alternating in various hues, offer a distinctive harlequin motif. Triangles are used to create chevron patterns, while octagons allow for the introduction of a contrasting tile or decorative insert. Shape and size are not the only aspects that contribute to pattern; color can work visual magic as well, creating checkerboards, ginghams, plaids, pinstripes, tumbling blocks, and a variety of random looks.

Not only does pattern add interest to a room, but it can also fool the eye into thinking its dimensions are different. Quite often, a bold pattern will make a room look smaller, while a large butt-jointed tile in a solid shade will extend the visual expanse. In addition to size, shape, and color, the interplay of light and dark, soft and rough, and glossy and matte will offer significant interest as well. Pattern is a product of contrast and juxtaposition of varying material qualities, which in the end is what creates the illusion. Don't allow your design to overwhelm a space or compete with adjacent elements. Use pattern to your advantage; induce excitement, not headaches.

Tile Patterns

Texture and finish. Texture and finish combine to form a surface layer we can savor both visually and through our sense of touch. When it comes to tile, textures range from butter soft and smooth to rugged and rough. These textures affect the overall character of a tile, which in turn affects its final appearance once installed. A rough, matte-finish tile will instill a relaxed and casual mood, while a glossy tile will appear more formal and elegant. Shiny finishes emphasize clear brilliant color, and matte finishes tone it down. Sparkling streamlined surfaces tend to make dirt more obvious; tiles with varied color and texture will camouflage it.

Texture is also evident in the way a tile is made. Handmade tiles are lovingly irregular; machine-milled pieces are uniform and precise. In addition to glossy and matte, we see satin, brushed, rippled, ribbed, iridescent, crackled, wavy, mottled, streaked, sandy, pooled, and variegated surfaces and each imparts it own unique style.

Trims and borders. Trims and borders are specialty tiles that work in conjunction with field tiles to create a clean, finished look. Trims, either surface or radius, are generally used for practical purposes such as capping exposed edges and making neat transitions to other materials, whereas borders are more decorative in nature. Within the realm of border

TERMS   tile patterns

diagonal: Tile is set at a 45-degree angle to the wall.
square: Tile is set at a 90-degree angle to the wall.
offset: Square tiles are set in a staggered pattern.
herringbone: Tiles are set in adjoining vertical rows of slanting lines, in which two adjacent lines form a **V** or inverted **V**.
checkerboard: Square tiles alternate in differing shades to create a checkerboard pattern.
modular: A distinctive Old World pattern formed by placing together tiles of differing sizes and shapes.
random: Tiles of various sizes and shapes are set in an undetermined pattern.
bordered: Strips of field tile, or contrasting colored tile, are used to create a border, whether to outline a room or to create a carpet effect.
brick style: Rectangular tiles are staggered, like bricks in a wall.
octagonal: Clipping all four corners of a square tile results in an octagon; a decorative accent or contrasting "dot" can be inserted between these tiles.
basket weave: Rectangular tiles are set in a pattern that mimics woven material.
crisscross: Square tiles are bordered on all four sides with contrasting material of a smaller width, resulting in a crisscross pattern when repeated through a room.

tiles, you will find beautiful deep-relief braided ropes, strings of pearls, swirling vines, acanthus leaves, and thick crown moldings, just to name a few. Borders (also referred to as liners or listellos) appear more prominent in the design, rather than blending in with field tiles; often they are the feature that can make your design sing. You can opt to stack them, blend variations in size, relief, and pattern, create a picture-frame effect, or use them as architectural details, as with a baseboard, chair rail, and crown molding combination.

Most mass-produced ceramic and porcelain lines come with a bevy of coordinating trims to complete the job. However, many handmade and specialty lines do not. When the trim tiles you require are not available, you can count on a little ingenuity or a talented installer to compensate. Standard field tiles can be rounded over, mitered, or layered to complete the look. If this option does not appeal to you, consider finishing off the exposed edges with decorative wood borders or complementing trims from other tile lines.

Common Trim Pieces

Angle tiles negotiate inside and outside corners.
Base tiles are used as a baseboard on a floor when no tile will be placed above them.
A **bead** is a convex molding used to turn an outside corner.
Bullnose tiles are flat tiles rounded over on one or more sides to create a soft finished edge; they are commonly placed at the end of a row of field tiles.
Coves are concave tiles used to turn corners at a right angle.
A **half-round** is a semi-cylindrical trim tile used primarily for decoration.
Quarter-round tiles are used to negotiate 90-degree angles where a horizontal surface meets a vertical surface.
A **radius bullnose** is similar to a surface bullnose, but has a more substantial curve so that it can

wrap over an underlying or protruding substrate. A **V-cap**, used on the front edge of a countertop, often features a curved depression to contain spills.

Floors. Everything comes into play to formulate the ideal floor, from size and shape to color and pattern and you don't have to break the bank to create a beautiful design. A sense of style conveyed through the use of pattern—a matter of sitting down with a pencil and graph paper—might be all you need . Something as simple as a contrasting border can make a big statement. Borders can be placed right against the wall to create a shadow effect, or inset by a foot or two for an entirely different look. If you love the idea of placing your floor on the diagonal but feel overwhelmed by all the cuts, choose to border the room with a full or half tile placed square against the wall, and then fill the center with the diagonal pattern. A well-chosen border width can minimize the number of cuts and maximize the use of material at the same time. You can also choose to create smaller, more intricate designs that mimic throw rugs. These inlaid tile designs often function as the room's focal point, and are best placed in areas where you can enjoy them such as the foyer, hallway, dining room, and powder bath. When creating a tile "throw rug," begin by making a template to minimize your cuts and waste. Set the defining frame first. Once the boundaries of the frame are in place, find the center and work outward. Tile choices for a rug project can vary widely, depending upon the look you are trying to achieve. For more detail, fill the interior space with a tile that contrasts with your border and field tile in size, color, shape, or finish, or all four for even

RIGHT: Mosaic accents placed at the intersection of four marble tiles create a pinwheel effect. The result is a stunning, classic composition.

OPPOSITE: This painstakingly handcrafted mosaic floor mimics the look of autumn leaves that have just fallen to the ground.

more intrigue. If you are working within a limited budget, create the border from the field tiles themselves and fill the center by altering its size and pattern.

In an open-floor-plan home, tile offers the perfect solution for delineating an uninterrupted flow from room to room and from the inside out. It can also mark transitions between spaces through a change of size or pattern, or addition of a decorative or contrasting border. Avoid using entirely different materials in each room, which can lead to a patchwork-quilt look that disturbs the desired calming rhythm.

When selecting material for your floor, consider the objects that float above it. If you are working around dramatic artwork, area rugs, upholstered furniture, drapery, and cabinetry, it is wise to select a tile that will lie quietly and not fight for attention. If you want to make your flooring itself the room's focal point, on the other hand, tone down all other surrounding elements and let the tile take center stage.

It takes a little practice, but strong visualization skills are necessary to envision the finished product. Close your eyes and imagine the big picture and how it will all work together. If necessary, create a design board that features small swatches of each item intended to occupy the finished area. Objects in a room must give and take, alternating between the roles of focus and backdrop, if the space is to work. Keeping all of this in mind, feel free to express your individuality and personal style. Your home is a reflection of you.

Bathrooms. Bathrooms are the perfect forums to display your creativity. Because they are entities unto themselves, you can be bold with

their design. Safety must take top priority, however; before formulating your plan, choose a floor tile with substantial texture, to avoid any possible slip hazards. In the shower, large flush-cut tiles set tightly together will minimize grout joints in turn, minimizing future maintenance. On tub surrounds and showers that do not extend to the ceiling, consider capping the tile with a substantial crown molding in lieu of the standard surface or radius bullnose. Adding a decorative border or listello is well worth the investment and can take a basic bathroom from conventional to spectacular. In master bathroom applications that feature a separate shower and whirlpool tub, use the same design elements in each area—for example, the

same border found in the shower can serve as a backsplash for the tub. To add texture and dimension, create a mosaic in the shower niche, and use a deep relief molding as its frame. Take a close look at each individual feature of the bathroom (the vanity, mirror, tub, shower, floor, walls and ceiling) and add dramatic architectural detail through the use of tile. Because bathrooms are not wide open spaces, you can add plenty of pizzazz without blowing your budget

Countertops. One of the biggest drawbacks of tile countertops in the past were the grout joints. Wide grout lines are hard to keep clean, tending to become unsightly and unsanitary. Today, however, tiles are produced in much larger sizes, and flush-cut edges allow them to be tightly set, avoiding these problems. Tile now can be an ideal option for countertops, combining affordability with do-it-yourself ease and offering an endless array of options.

Backsplashes. In the grand scheme of things, the backsplash comprises a very small area within the kitchen,

RIGHT: Saturated black mosaics surround a white soaking tub. Such stark contrasts in materials can create a very graphic and visually exciting outcome.

but oh, what an important area! Because the splash is often the first thing you see upon entering the space, it is important to devote plenty of time to its design.

On average, the space between a countertop and the bottom portion of the wall cabinet falls between sixteen and eighteen inches. Increasing this area slightly, to twenty, twenty-two, or even twenty-four inches, dramatically alters the impact of the splash and expands your options significantly. Once you have cre-

LEFT: This bathroom fuses beauty, the safety of slip resistance and ease of maintinance to arrive at the ultimate marriage of form and function.

edge of the cabinetry, or install outlets on the undersides of the cabinets themselves. Lastly, you may place receptacles at the very bottom of the splash, horizontally instead of vertically, to make them less noticeable.

If you're planning a picture-frame design or mural as a focal point, it might be a good idea to cut out a template on kraft paper and place it in the intended location. Leave the room, then walk back in and give it the "glance treatment." You will know right away if your design is in the correct scale. Make any adjust-

ated a larger canvas on which to work, you can begin dreaming up a variety of unique configurations.

When you have arrived at an initial concept, do the math. Map out your design on graph paper, and be sure you know where the last tile will be placed before you set the first. Remember— symmetry is the key to a visually successful back-splash. Know where outlets and switch plates will fall, and make accommodations for them within the design. Better yet, attempt to keep these receptacles outside the design entirely; for example, consider placing an outlet strip at the top of the splash, where it will be hidden by the lower

ments, and try again until you are satisfied. The ideal place for such a feature is in the stove, back-splash, and vent hood combination. Often, this layout offers a little extra height, and this trio can become the featured focal point of your kitchen design. If you are not using a premade vent hood but building a frame to be tiled, be sure to pull up a prominent feature from your splash and place it on the hood as well, to tie the two together.

When planning your splash, don't limit yourself to the customary flat layout. Think three-dimensional by introducing something that is eye-catching and useful. These special details are generally located

just behind the cooking surface or above the sink. An arched, recessed niche can provide the perfect display space for a unique collection of objects or a elegantly framed piece of artwork. When adding a niche, consider bordering it with ornate trim and lining its interior with colorful micro-mosaics or something unexpected. Ledges above the sink can hold colorful glass bottles filled with vegetables or pots of herbs for the gourmet cook. Another way to add dimension to your spash is through the incorporation of high profile trim pieces. By blending thick ogee or bullnose trims with tiles that offer an interesting texture, you can create a splash that will literally reach out and grab your attention.

Finally, when designing your backsplash, take into consideration the colors and patterns found in all of the surrounding elements—floors, walls, countertops, the vent hood, appliances, fixtures, and cabinetry. The splash can serve to tie the entire space together by reflecting the colors found throughout the room. Always remember the rule of give and take. Be sure to balance elements such as color and pattern wisely. The last thing you want to do is make everything a dramatic focal point and have all of your efforts result in a dizzying space. When in doubt, a design board can come to the rescue, as can a detailed drawing of your space on graph paper. You should notice pretty quickly if elements are antagonizing one another. Making adjustments at this planning stage will save you from living with expensive mistakes later.

Fireplaces. The natural focal point in many a room, a fireplace can easily become a star feature when wrapped with tile. Fireplace style depends largely on the style of the home in which it resides. A Mediterranean-inspired dwelling calls for large, ornately detailed cast or carved stone surrounds, whereas a contemporary interior requires only a clean-lined geometric facade. Because the fireplace surround represents a relatively small surface area, you may want to consider stretching your budget somewhat to transform it into something special. Mix materials—stone and glass, or concrete and metal. Decorative mosaic borders are ideal for simply tracing the outside of the box itself. Handmade artist tiles are wonderful on the face of the fireplace; these can be pricey in mass, but you don't need all that many to create an impressive display here.

OPPOSITE: A trio of hand-painted panels are traced with dark polished mosaics. The field tile is beveled four-by-eight-inch bricks of Dore Royale marble.

LEFT: A blue and white Tunisian tile design is framed by slabs of travertine creating this spectacular focal point.

When choosing tiles for your fireplace, consider not only the surround of the firebox itself, but the hearth and over-mantel area as well, as yet more opportunity to create interest.

Stairs. Stairs, due to their imposing proportions, also create a natural focal point, and as with any large-scale feature, they offer a chance to convey a certain style through the incorporation of well-thought-out materials. Formal grandeur can be generated though by cladding the stairs with a timeless classic such as Carrara marble. In a zesty Mediterranean abode, risers may be faced with hand-painted tiles of bright yellow, cobalt blue, and dusty terra-cotta. If your home reflects an Old World ambience, then soft shades of limestone or travertine will enhance the effect.

Areas of stairways that are most visible should get the most attention. Risers can sport beautifully handcrafted tiles, while the tread's front edge can be dressed with a heavy bullnose trim to make each step appear more substantial. Lastly, don't overlook landings. These normally undecorated areas can be enhanced through a mosaic or hand-crafted inlaid medallion. It is these little details that make all the difference.

Mixed media. With so many different tiles from which to fashion a wonderfully eccentric look in and about the home, you may opt to take things a step further and weave various materials together for yet another layer of excitement. From the traditional look of terra-cotta tile set between crisscrossing pickets of wood to more unexpected blends of semiprecious stones placed at the juncture of reflective marble tiles, there are never-ending possibilities. When you head to the tile shop, layer a limestone tile against a sheet of glistening glass

mosaic and toss in a handful of lustrous metal decos, then see if your creative juices don't start flowing. Just keep in mind, when mixing things up, that each element may require its own setting method and care, so be certain it is a combination you can live with.

Little details. When considering where in your home you want to incorporate tile, don't overlook the less obvious areas. Project this special treatment onto walls as wainscoting, or place it between heavy aged wooden beams overhead. Use tiles in place of standard wood molding, and frame doorways and windows with their beauty. Small architectural details, such as a window seat, can be tiled, as well as the windowsill itself. Of course this versatile material is right at home in the great outdoors—the perfect addition to porches, patios, and pools. Imagine a secret courtyard with a large tiled fountain or an ornate outdoor shower with a beautiful pebble mosaic underfoot. Very few elements in the home cannot benefit in one way or another from tile. Get creative—go tile crazy!

ABOVE: By dressing risers with decorative tiles and mosaics an ordinary stairway becomes magical.

OPPOSITE: A ledge behind the kitchen sink offers a great space to display glass jars of vegetables and pots of herbs.

Creating Style with Tile

Many facets are involved in creating style in a home. Each piece of the interior design puzzle must be scrutinized and well thought out if we are to achieve the desired look. All too often, when we're building or remodeling a home, budget limitations become most apparent toward the end of the project. Unfortunately, this affects the final layers of design, the things we see each and every day. Commonly, prominent focal areas such as flooring, counter-tops, backsplashes, vent hoods, fireplaces, stairways, and bathrooms end up bearing the brunt of an effort to save money, thus resulting in a bland and boring look. If you are building new or taking on an extensive remodel, be sure to formulate a plan that leaves room in the budget for these essential finishing touches. In the chart below, you will discover tiles that help achieve specific styles. By spending wisely and planning well ahead of time, you will be able to weave stunning materials into one-of-a-kind designs that will make your home a showplace. It is this attention to detail that will leave your home brimming with character, and make your guests green with envy.

STYLES	TILES	IDEAS
Old World	<ul><li>Random patterned distressed travertine, limestone, and marble</li><li>Oversize stamped and weathered concrete pavers made to resemble natural stone</li><li>Any ceramic or porcelain tile that appears aged, worn, chipped, pitted, or chiseled</li><li>Mosaics</li><li>Large parquet tiles</li><li>Aged hand-painted or carved tile</li><li>Metal accents with a rustic patina</li></ul>	<ul><li>Select a very old-looking stone, such as a dark unfilled travertine with a chiseled edge, in a random pattern for floors.</li><li>Consider a honed or brushed stone—perhaps travertine, limestone, marble, or granite—for countertops.</li><li>Choose a rustic field tile for the splash, and insert metal accents with an aged patina.</li><li>Stick with earthy natural colors such as walnut, wheat, cocoa, and cream.</li></ul>
English Cottage	<ul><li>Dark rugged slate</li><li>Antiquated stone</li><li>Brick</li><li>Parquet</li><li>Encaustic tile</li><li>Medieval tile</li><li>Soapstone</li><li>Porcelain and ceramic that mimic aged natural materials</li><li>English delftware tile</li><li>Hand-painted garden scenes, with roses, herbs, and wildflowers</li></ul>	<ul><li>Incorporate slate or brick in a deep rich color for floors.</li><li>For countertops, choose something soft and matte in finish, such as soapstone, honed marble, or limestone.</li><li>On the backsplash, contrast dark countertops with light-colored tiles complete with hand-painted accents of potted herbs and garden motifs. Stencil the names of herbs such as rosemary, thyme, and sage across several of the tiles.</li><li>Keep the color palette muted and earthy.</li></ul>

STYLES	TILES	IDEAS
French Country	• Reclaimed terra-cotta • Parquet in large latticework panels or in herringbone or chevron patterns • Antiquated travertine or limestone • Wood, stone, or terra-cotta porcelain look-alikes • Hand-painted murals • Colorful glazed tiles • Blue-and-white tiles	• Seek out authentic reclaimed French terra-cotta for floors. Set rectangular tiles in a herringbone pattern. • Blend thick wooden butcher block and subtle natural stone on countertops. • On the splash, feature a hand-painted mural of a pastoral scene such as a farm or vineyard. • Consider tiles with a distinct French motif, such as clusters of grapes or vintage wine names. • Blend earthy colors with bright shades of blue, red, yellow, and green.
Tuscan Farmhouse	• Terra-cotta set in a staggered brick or herringbone fashion • Concrete tiles that emulate terra-cotta pavers or aged stone • Antiquated stone • Rusticated brick • Porcelain tile that emulates antiquated stone or terra-cotta	• Use large irregular stone pavers or antiquated terra-cotta on the floor. • Cover the countertop with aged stone tiles. • Incorporate rustic tile on the splash, with accents that speak of Tuscany, such as hand-painted topiaries, olives, grapes, or wildflowers. • Use muted hues of ocher yellow, sienna, burnt umber, rust, and sage.
Mediterranean Villa	• Terra-cotta • Saltillo • Terra-cotta mixed with aged wood • Antiquated stone • Porcelain or ceramic that closely resembles natural materials • Vibrantly colored glazed tile • Hand-painted Spanish, Malibu, and majolica tiles • Blue-and-white Portuguese tiles	• On the floor, inset aged terra-cotta tile between crisscrossing pickets of distressed wood. Also consider antiquated stone with clipped corners, using brightly painted tiles as accents • Dress backsplashes, vent hoods, and stair risers with colorful hand-painted tiles that blend bright white, cobalt blue, sunshine yellow, and rusty red.

STYLES	TILES	IDEAS
Classic	• Parquet • Dark slate • Marble • Soapstone • Limestone • Accent tiles and borders with classic detailing • Subway brick tile • Porcelain hexagon tile • Delftware—English or Dutch	• Choose a timeless marble such as Carrara, Calcutta, or statuary for floors and stairs. Consider a black-and-white checkerboard design. • Use accent tiles with classic motifs such as egg-and-dart, acanthus leaf, Greek key, and dentil for floors and walls. • In the bath, choose marble or a white porcelain subway brick tile and hexagonal mosaic combination.
Contemporary	• Concrete • Leather • Glass • Metal • Vibrantly colored rubber tile • Porcelain in large squares • Sleek ceramics • Dark geometric parquet • Large limestone tiles • Solid colored slate • Porcelain tiles with a textile or fabric motif • Long, narrow rectangular tiles	• Choose large solid-colored tiles set with a tight grout joint for a seamless look. • Consider placing long, narrow rectangular tiles side by side. • Incorporate shiny surfaces such as polished stone, metal, and glass for sparkle. • Stick with clean lines and strict geometric patterns. • Use colors of soft slate blue, khaki green, sea grass beige, mushroom, and charcoal.
Rustic Cabin	• Slate • Aged stone • Random flagging • Leather tile • Terra-cotta • Art tile that depicts the outdoors • Embossed metal tile	• Choose dark, rugged aged natural stone for floors • Place leather tiles in special rooms of the house, such as the home office or study. • Accent with tiles that speak of the Wild West or the great outdoors, such as moose, bear, and elk. • Choose tile colors that reflect nature, such as berry red, evergreen, bark, moss, and oak.

STYLES	TILES	IDEAS
Romantic	• Limestone • Pillowed or cushioned stone • Porcelain or ceramic in soft feminine colors • Linoleum in a barely-there checker-board pattern • Parquet in a herringbone or chevron • Frosted glass in soft pastel hues • Monochromatic earth-toned ceramic and porcelain • Limestone or travertine • Cork that resembles travertine or leather	• Cover the floor with a slightly pillowed tile in butter yellow, blush pink, or ivory. • Accent with delicate etched, carved, or stenciled borders. • Consider colors of chocolate, plum, raspberry, or peach for countertops. • Accent the backsplash with romantic tiles of roses, wildflowers, and strings of pearls. • Create arched, rounded, and curvaceous focal points. • Place an ornately framed oil painting or deep-relief plaque on the splash as your focal point. • Include hand-painted or computer-generated tile murals of artwork from Romantic period artists.
Arts & Crafts	• Ceramic in traditional colors and matte finishes • Decorative tiles that evoke the Arts and Crafts period • Brick • Cork • Slate • Soapstone • Hammered metal • Random stone • Bachelor tiles • William De Morgan tiles • Tube-lined Art Nouveau tiles	• Consider black slate or dark brick for the floors. • Feature a large fireplace of stacked random stone or staggered brick. • Use a matte finished stone, such as slate or soapstone, for countertops. • Dress the backsplash with tiles depicting nature including animals, insects, pastoral scenes, and wildflowers. • Keep colors quiet and earthy—sage, olive, gold, russet, and shades of brown.
Victorian	• Modern encaustic tiles • Concrete tile that emulates the colorful and highly geometric modern encaustic look • William De Morgan tiles • Gothic tiles • Transfer-printed tiles in delicate floral designs • Tube-lined tiles • Colorful painted tile panels	• Consider a colorful geometric encaustic tile pattern for the floor. • Treat your backsplash to the highly detailed art tile popular in the Victorian era, or use a metal tile that resembles embossed tin. • In the bath, dress up plain white tiles with beautiful floral accents and borders.

PROJECT 1

Big, small, smooth, rough, flat, raised, glossy, matte, colorful, subdued, solid, patterned . . . these are just a handful of the words that can be used to describe the range of decorative tiles on the market today. Artistic tiles are bountiful, available in just about every configuration you can imagine. If you can dream it, most likely you can find it. What is so wonderful about all of this amazing diversity is that there is truly no ceiling placed on creativity, and formulating an individual style that showcases one's personality is as easy as can be. Some of these delectable decorative tiles are surprisingly easy on the pocketbook; in mass quantities, however, the mounting cost may curb your enthusiasm quite quickly. Therefore, when budget restraints damper your lofty vision, don't toss your ideas out the window entirely; just rely on a little ingenuity. In this chapter, we feature eight quick and easy tile projects anyone can do at home. Each project can be expanded upon; when you introduce your own unique ideas, the possibilities are endless. Soon you will learn how to produce tiles that mimic the look of metal, embossed tin, and colorful textiles. You will become familiar with basics that offer the foundation upon which to create a one-of-a-kind masterpiece. Have fun experimenting with size, pattern, color, texture, and finish. There are no rules—express yourself!

Materials

- Tumbled stone tiles or white ceramic tiles
- Pencil
- Acrylic paint (for stone tiles)
- Liquitex Glossies (for ceramic tiles)
- Paintbrush
- Plastic bag
- Small sponge
- Cup of water
- Rag

Step 1. Before choosing the stone tiles (here we refer to painting stone tiles, but the procedure is the same if you paint ceramic tiles) for your project, determine their intended use within the overall design, including their scale and how they will look once placed among the accompanying field tiles. For example, four-inch squares will work nicely in a field of similar four-inch tumbled stone tiles, and so on. However, there are no hard-and-fast rules; simply use your judgment and carefully plan your layout. Consider whether you require a single tile to obtain the desired effect, or if a set of three or four best suits your design needs. Once you have decided on the size, color, scale, and configuration of your tile, it is time to plan your motif.

Step 2. Take time to study other hand-painted tiles and get an idea of exactly what you would like to accomplish, whether abstract, whimsical, floral, or geometric. Gather all of your materials and experiment either on paper or on a sample tile first.

Step 3. With a pencil, lightly sketch your design on the tile or set of tiles. If you make a mistake or need to fine-tune the drawing, simply wash away any marks with a damp rag. Once you're satisfied with your outline, it is time to paint. There are a variety of paints from which to choose, and much depends on the final application of your tile. Ideally, delicate hand-painted tiles will be affixed to the wall, not the floor, and will be placed in dry, not wet, areas. In this case, most any craft paint will suffice. We used acrylic paint for our project.

Step 4. Begin by painting your creation with a brush. Remember, you can vary the shade of the primary colors with the addition of a bit of black or white paint. By adjusting the color shade up and down, you will introduce light, shadow, and dimension to your work. Creative effects can be accomplished by bunching up a small plastic bag and pouncing lightly as needed, or by using a small sponge to feather and soften edges.

Step 5. Once you have finished painting your tiles, allow them to dry completely. Be sure to take great care during the installation process, especially when grouting, so your artwork is not damaged. Taping a small piece of plastic over your design will help ensure that it does not get washed away. If you must seal your tiles, do so carefully by spraying them lightly with a water-based sealer made for natural stone. There is no need to seal ceramic tiles; however, you can opt to apply a layer or two of clear ceramic enamel (available at craft stores) for added protection. Just be certain the paint is completely dry, and practice on a sample piece first. When you choose to use Liquitex Glossies paint on ceramic, the tile design is baked on and can withstand greater wear.

Materials

- Two-inch square ceramic tiles—netted or individual
- Appliqué (if making your own appliqué, flexible molds and clay)
- Adhesive (strong glue)
- Metallic paint
- Sponge brush

Step 1. Gather materials. If you purchased netted ceramic tiles, cut them from the sheet and clean them well. If you decided to make your own appliqués rather than buying them premade, you must mold the clay the day before your project so that it has sufficient time to harden. For our project, we used a small decorative rubber mold and self-hardening clay from the local craft store.

Step 2. After your clay appliqué has hardened, affix it to the tile with strong glue. Allow time for it to dry completely.

Step 3. Paint the ceramic tile and affixed appliqué with the metallic paint you've chosen, using a sponge brush. Allow to dry. Note: The specialty paint used in this project is actual liquid metal, available in silver, copper, bronze, and antiquated finishes of copper patina and rust. We purchased our metal paint at a local craft store.

Step 4. Once they have dried, use the metallic tiles as accents on your backsplash, vent hood, or any area that does not experience direct water exposure or heavy traffic. Mix them with stone tile, glass mosaics, or ceramic field tiles. Use your imagination to create even more unique designs, including metal trims and borders.

PROJECT 3

Materials

- Four-by-four-inch tumbled stone tiles
- Metal, plastic, or handmade stencil
- Tape
- Stencil brush or sponge brush
- Acrylic paint or spray paint

Step 1. Gather materials. Center stencil on the tile carefully and tape it in place securely.

Step 2. Load your brush with paint; do not saturate the brush, however, as you do not want the paint to bleed under the stencil.

Pounce over the stencil with the brush until you've obtained even coverage. You may also choose to lightly spray the stencil with spray paint, as long as you have sufficiently taped off all areas that do not require paint.

Step 3. Allow paint to dry slightly, and carefully remove the stencil.

Step 4. Once dry, use your tile in low-traffic areas.

Materials

- Tile (stone or ceramic)
- Paint
- Paintbrush
- Tray for paint
- Stamp
- Tape
- Pencil

Step 1. Gather materials. Center the stamp on your tile and either mark or tape reference lines to ensure your design is centered.

Step 2. Press your stamp into the paint, then carefully stamp the image on the tile with light pressure. Be careful not to let the stamp slide in any direction. Lift the stamp.

Step 3. If you are not satisfied with the look of your design, feel free to fill in light areas with your paintbrush.

Step 4. Allow the paint to dry completely, then place tile in a low-traffic area. For an aged, distressed look, once the paint is completely dry, lightly sand the stamped image with sandpaper to remove a portion of the paint.

Materials

- Four-by-four-inch white ceramic tile with matte finish
- Decorative embossed metallic paper from craft store
- Foam sponge brush
- Decoupage medium
- Tray for decoupage
- Scissors

Step 1. Gather materials. Set the tile on the decorative paper and, with a pencil, trace an outline just slightly bigger than the tile itself. Cut out the paper, following the penciled outline.

Step 2. Pour a small amount of decoupage medium into a cup, tray, or terra-cotta saucer. Using a foam sponge brush, apply the decoupage medium evenly to the face of the white tile as well as on all four sides.

Step 3. Place the decorative square of paper on the tile; press lightly to ensure good adhesion across the entire face of the tile and on all four sides, where the paper slightly overlaps.

Step 4. Allow to dry completely. Use your decorative embossed tile on any vertical surface, as an

accent or in mass. Consider using this technique with different sizes of tiles, as well as for trims and borders.

Materials

- Four-by-four-inch white ceramic tile in matte finish
- Decorative paper from craft store
- Foam sponge brush
- Decoupage medium
- Tray
- Scissors
- Pencil

Step 1. Gather materials. Set the tile on the decorative paper and, with a pencil, trace an outline just slightly bigger than the tile itself. Cut out the paper, following the penciled outline.

Step 2. Pour a small amount of decoupage medium into a cup, tray, or terra-cotta saucer. Using a foam sponge brush, apply the decoupage medium evenly to the face of the white tile, as well as on all four sides.

Step 3. Place the decorative square of paper on the tile; press lightly to ensure good adhesion across the entire face of the tile and on all four sides, where the paper slightly overlaps.

Step 4. With the foam sponge brush, apply an even coat of decoupage medium to the decorative paper for added protection. If desired, more than one coat can be applied. In place of the decoupage medium, you may consider a topcoat of clear ceramic enamel, available at craft stores.

Step 5. Allow to dry completely. Use your decorative tile on any vertical surface, as an accent or in mass. Consider using this technique with different sizes of tiles, as well as for trims and borders.

Materials

- Four-by-four-inch tumbled stone tiles
- Rice paper
- Decoupage medium
- Foam sponge brush
- Tray
- Scissors
- Cup of water

Step 1. Select an image to be printed on the rice paper. Adjust the image size to fit the tile, either on your computer or by adjusting its size on a Xerox machine. Print the image.

Step 2. Cut out the image. If desired, carefully tear the edges of the rice paper for an aged or irregular look. If needed, wet your fingertips lightly to tear paper.

Step 3. Apply a coat of decoupage medium to the face of the stone tile with a foam sponge brush. Place the image on the face of the tile. Allow to dry.

Step 4. Once dry, apply another coat or two of decoupage medium for surface protection. Allow to dry.

Step 5. Use your picture tiles in low-traffic areas.

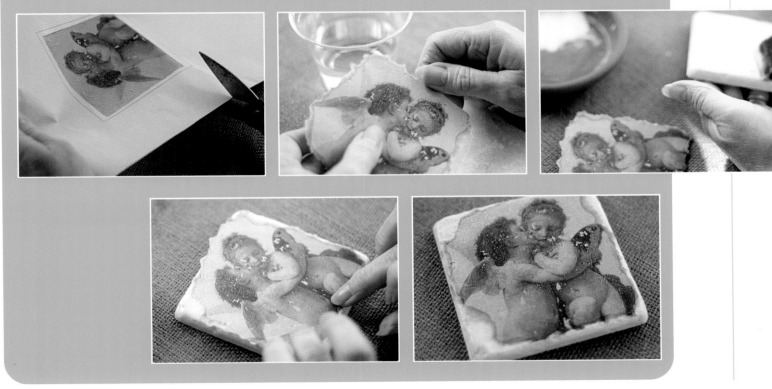

PROJECT 8

Materials

- White Portland cement
- Fine white sand
- Plaster
- Concrete stain (what ever color you desire; we used brown)
- Antiquing liquid (brown, or any color you wish)
- Premade plastic tile molds, available on-line on eBay; or make your own
- Two mixing buckets
- Measuring cup
- Soy oil for mold release
- Sponge brush
- Mixing tool or wooden spoon
- Gloves

Step 1. Gather all of your materials. Apply the soy oil release to your plastic molds so you will not have to go back and do so later.

Step 2. Mix all dry ingredients in a container. The size of your job will determine the amount of concrete mixture you make at a given time. The mixture sets up quickly, so the smaller the batch, the better. For our tiles, we used one cup white Portland cement, one cup plaster, and one cup white sand to one cup water.

Step 3. Pour water into a separate container, and mix in color. Concentrated concrete pigment goes a long way, so a tiny bit will do. We used an eighth of a teaspoon. You can also tint your water with antiquing liquid, or substitute coffee for a nice light brown coloration (be aware that the color of the mix does not reflect the final color of the tile once cured).

Step 4. Slowly sift and stir the dry ingredients into the colored water. The final mixture should be similar to thick cake batter or well-whipped frosting. If the mixture seems too dry, add a little more water until you can easily pour it into the molds.

Step 5. Pour the wet mixture into molds that have been treated with the soy oil release. If the mixture is very thick, use a margin trowel or putty knife to scoop it out and press it into the molds. Fill each mold flush to the top.

Step 6. Place your molds where they will not be disturbed, and where the temperature is not too cold. Ideally the temperature should remain above 50 degrees for adequate curing. Allow the tiles to set up in the molds a minimum of twelve hours, ideally twenty-four.

Step 7. Once the concrete has cured, carefully loosen the molds by twisting lightly from side to side. Turn the mold over on a soft rag and shake gently to allow the tile to fall from the mold.

Step 8. If desired, you can age the tiles' surfaces by applying brown antiquing liquid, available at local craft stores.

Step 9. These concrete tiles are very delicate, and are recommended for wall applications only. Concrete floor tiles can be made in much the same way, but require a much thicker mold to survive underfoot. Until the concrete tiles and trims have been installed, be gentle with them. Once they are set in place with mortar, they will be very durable. You should seal the tiles with a penetrating sealer if they will be used in areas prone to splashes and spills.

part IV | **installation**

TILE SETTING TOOLS

Before the 1950s, ceramic and natural stone tile was set using a thick bed of mortar reinforced with metal lath, an exhausting process that required an experienced professional to do the job. As the years have passed and more advanced and simplified tiling methods have been introduced, the art of setting tile is now well within the realm of possibility for the average homeowner. Lighter and thinner tile, plywood, backer board, specialty underlayments, thinset mortar, and innovative tools have all helped ease the installation of this versatile material. The goal of this chapter is to acquaint you with the tools required to do a professional job and the general skills you need to get you started on your way. After digesting this information, you will be ready to move on to the projects featured in the following three chapters, confident in your knowledge, whether you are a budding pro or simply a weekend warrior.

Understanding Tile Substrates

It is well known in the tile world that an installation is only as good as what lies beneath it. Significant time should be spent inspecting and preparing the area you wish to tile. Be sure that substrates are in good repair, clean, dry, sturdy, plumb, level, and strong enough to bear the weight of the tile. Many novice tile setters are surprised at the substantial amount of time that must be devoted to substrate preparation, but don't let this discourage you. A well-prepared foundation for your project will ensure a long-lasting and trouble-free

For Room and Substrate Preparation

- **Angle grinder**, for scoring cement backer board
- **Carbide scriber**, also used for scoring cement backer board
- **Circular saw**, for cutting plywood and scoring cement backer board
- **Drill**, for removing screws and securing underlayments such as plywood and cement backer board
- **Drywall knife**, for repairing drywall
- **Fiberglass mesh tape**, for taping joints in backer board/other
- **Handsaw**, for cutting wooden trim, moldings, and casings, and for trimming doors
- **Hacksaw**, for cutting metal
- **Hammer**, for demolition and nailing
- **Hammer and chisel**, for removing old tile
- **Jamb saw**, for trimming molding around doors
- **Jigsaw**, for cutting out holes in plywood
- **Plastic and tape**, to tape off other rooms and lessen dust exposure during demolition
- **Pry bar**, for removing molding, trim, baseboards, shoe mold, tack strips, thresholds, shower surrounds, and old flooring
- **Putty knife**, for removing old flaking paint, adhesives, caulk, and other difficult-to-remove debris
- **Razor blade scraper**, also used to remove old paint, glue, wallpaper, tile adhesive, and other stubborn remnants from floors and walls
- **Screwdriver**, for removing fixtures
- **Screws and nails**, for securing loose wooden boards, and to adhere new underlayments such as plywood and cement backer board
- **Stud finder**, for locating studs in walls and joists in floors
- **Sander**, for removal of stubborn debris from floors and walls
- **Utility knife**, for cutting carpet, vinyl, and linoleum, loosening caulk, and scoring cement backer board
- **Wrenches**, for loosening plumbing and removing sinks and toilets

For Planning the Layout

- **Carpenter's square**, for making mitered and angled cuts.

- **Chalk**, for snapping working lines and grids
- **Framing square**, for marking angles and drawing straight lines
- **Jury stick**, for planning layout, measuring, and maintaining correct tile spacing
- **Level**, to assess substrates for plumb and level; can also be used as a straightedge
- **Pencil**, for marking lines
- **Straightedge**, for keeping tile edges straight and marking straight lines
- **Tape measure**

For Cutting Tile

- **Angle grinder**, for dry-cutting masonry, ceramic, stone, and cement backer board
- **Grease pen** or permanent marker, for marking tiles to be cut with a wet saw
- **Hole saw**, for drilling holes in tile for pipes and plumbing
- **Nippers or biters**, for making irregularly shaped cuts on ceramic tile
- **Rubbing stone**, for softening rough edges on tile, stone, or cement backer board
- **Snap cutter**, for making straight cuts on ceramic tile
- **Wet saw**, for cutting natural stone and porcelain tile (can also be used to cut almost any type of tile)

For Setting Tile

- **Beater board and rubber mallet**, used to ensure even coverage across tile, particularly with netted mosaics
- **Five-gallon buckets**, for mixing setting materials, and to hold water for cleanup

- **Drill and mortar mixing paddles**, for mixing large amounts of materials such as thinset, grout, and self-leveling compounds
- **Levels**, to ensure a plumb and level installation
- **Margin trowels**, for mixing and scooping mortar, for back-buttering tiles, and to spread mortar in hard-to-reach places
- **Square or V-notched trowels**, for spreading mortar
- **Spacers**, to ensure equal grout joint spacing between tiles
- **Sponges and clean water**, for removing any mortar that may squeeze up between tiles, and to maintain a clean installation
- **Straightedge**, as a guide to keep tile courses straight
- **Wedges**, to shim vertical tiles

For Grouting Tile

- **Buckets**, for mixing grout and to hold water for removing excess grout and haze from the tile surface
- **Dry cloths**, for buffing grout haze from tile
- **Grout bag**, for grouting high-relief or decorative tiles that would be difficult to grout by the standard method
- **Grout float**, for forcing grout into joints and removing excess grout from tile surfaces
- **Margin trowel**, for mixing and scooping grout
- **Spacer removal tool**, for removing tile spacers prior to grouting
- **Sponges**, for removing excess grout from tile and to wipe away grout haze
- **Striking tools**, for smoothing grout joints for a finished appearance

For Sealing and Finishing Tile

- **Caulk and caulk gun**, for caulking expansion joints in the tile installation
- **Damp towels**, for cleaning and striking caulk joints
- **Lint-free soft cloth**, for wiping up excess sealer
- **Sealer and applicator**, for sealing grout joints and porous tile
- **Spray bottle**, for applying sealer to porous tile

For Cleanup

- **Broom**
- **Buckets**, to hold clean water
- **Clean cloths**, for general cleaning and grout haze removal
- **Industrial-strength vacuum or shop vac**, to remove large debris and heavy particles
- **Kraft paper and tape**, to protect finished floors and countertops during the remainder of the construction phase
- **Mop**
- **Putty knife and scrub brush**, for removing stuck-on dirt or dry mortar or grout from tile

Safety Equipment

- **Rubber gloves**
- **Work gloves**
- **Knee pads**
- **Safety glasses/goggles**
- **Ear protection**
- **Particle mask/respirator**
- **Back support**
- **Clean water**
- **First aid kit**

ing felt) and polyethylene (for example, 4-millimeter film, 30-millimeter chlorinated polyethylene, and the Schlüter Systems products Kerdi and Ditra), in addition to trowel-on membranes (with or without reinforcing fabric) and roll-on liquid membranes (like Custom's Red Guard). Because of the wide variety of options available, there is bound to be a product that suits both your skill level and budget, so there is no excuse not to adequately waterproof your tile installation. You will never regret that you did so.

Crack-isolation membranes. As with waterproof membranes, crack-isolation membranes are available in sheet form (like Schlüter Systems' Ditra), as well as trowel-on with fabric reinforcement (like Laticrete's Blue 92). The reason behind their use, as the name implies, is to prevent cracks in tile and grout caused by movement in the underlying substrate. Commonly used with concrete and plywood subfloors, these membranes do not guarantee that absolutely no cracking will ever occur, but they do reduce the risk considerably.

Other. Other membranes commonly used under tile include sound control and mud-bed-curing membranes, neither of which are routinely encountered by the average homeowner tackling small DIY projects.

Tile Adhesives and Trowels

Once your substrate has been well prepped, you must then select the correct adhesive, accompanied by the appropriate applicator (trowel), to arrive at the long-lasting results you desire. Using the correct setting method and material is yet another important step on the path to a trouble-free tile installation.

Adhesive is the material that physically bonds the tile to its substrate. It is important to use the correct setting material for your particular tile and

underlayment, as not all adhesives are appropriate in all situations. Some common adhesives:

Mastic. Premixed organic mastic is a popular adhesive, due in part to its ease of application and cost-effectiveness. It is composed of a bonding agent (latex or petroleum) combined with a carrier that eventually evaporates, allowing the tile to adhere to the substrate. Because it bonds in this unique manner, it is imperative that you do not use mastic that has begun to dry or harden within its container. In addition, be sure to work in small areas to prevent premature drying (skinning over), which will prevent the tile from adequately adhering to the substrate. Because of its strong grip when wet, you will find mastic commonly used in dry vertical installations, particularly over drywall and plywood. Although mastic is easy to use, it is not the ideal choice for many tile installations (mastic is not advised for floor installations or around fireboxes, for example). Thinset mortar (particularly modified thinset) provides a much better bond and increased flexibility, making it the better choice in most instances. In addition, mastic can yellow over time, something to consider when you're installing translucent tile such as glass or a porous material such as natural stone.

Thinset. By definition, thinset describes a particular method of setting tile; the term is also used to describe the mortar adhesive used during installation, however. Thinset mortar, in its basic form, is comprised primarily of Portland cement, sand, and a pinch of various other ingredients. This white or gray dry powder mixture is then blended with water to a creamy smooth consistency prior to setting the tile. Many installations call for the use of a modified thinset mortar, one that has been fortified with polymers such as latex or acrylic. Not long ago, liquid latex or acrylic was used in place of water to arrive at this formula, but most manufacturers now add these chemicals at the factory in dry powder form. Modified thinset mortar offers water resistance, greater working time, better bonding strength, and increased flexibility, thus addressing the poor performance issues, such as cracking or delaminating, often associated with tile. In addition to regular thinset and modified thinset, you will also find medium-bed mortar (marble and granite mix) and epoxy mortar. Medium-bed mortar is commonly used in when setting large, heavy, or irregular tiles such as natural stone, terra-cotta, and Saltillo, as it provides a thicker mortar base (up to three-quarters of an inch) upon which to set the tile. Epoxy thinset is employed when chemical resistance and/or superior bond strength is required. It is pricey and difficult to work with, but allows you to tile over such substrates as metal, glass, ceramic, resilient flooring, plywood, and other less than ideal surfaces. Whatever type of setting material you select, be sure to read and follow the manufacturer's directions, mix at the correct speed, and allow the mixture to slake for ten minutes before using.

Thinset mortar is available in white and gray. Use white if you are working with a light-colored stone or ceramic, or if you will be using a light-colored grout. Select the gray if you are working with dark tile or grout.

Trowel. A trowel is the tool used to comb uniform rows of adhesive (mastic or mortar) onto a substrate. The size and the type of trowel used varies; normally, the bigger and thicker the tile, the larger-notched trowel, and vice versa. The notch size (and overall depth of the adhesive) should equal approximately two-thirds the thickness of the tile being set (be sure to hold the trowel at slightly less than a 45-degree angle to the substrate when combing the adhesive). Another thing to consider when selecting a trowel size is the levelness of your substrate. If you are tiling a floor that is not perfectly level, selecting a trowel with larger

notches will make your job easier. Be aware that both too much or too little mortar can cause problems; the goal is to find the middle ground. Here are a few guidelines:

V-notched trowels. V-notched trowels range in size from one-eighth of an inch to a quarter inch; commonly used with mastic, they can also used to apply thinset. Use this type of trowel with small, lightweight tiles with smooth backs, such as glazed wall tiles, mosaic sheets, and glass.

Square-notched and U-shaped trowels. Square-notched and U-shaped trowels are most commonly used with larger, heavier floor and wall tiles set with thinset mortar (a very popular square-notched trowel being the one-quarter inch). When setting these larger tiles, be sure to pull up several to check for adequate mortar coverage. If the tile back is not well covered, you should consider using a trowel with larger notches. In these situations, you may also need to back- butter tiles to ensure proper mortar coverage. If the amount and depth of setting material is not sufficient, you run the risk of hollow spots and voids underneath the tile, where future cracks are likely to appear.

Choosing the Right Trowel

For mosaic sheets and small wall tile: Three-sixteenths- to quarter-inch V-notched trowel

For four-, six-, and eight-inch wall tile: Quarter-inch square-notched trowel

For eight- and twelve-inch floor and wall tile: One-quarter-by-three-eighths-inch square-notched trowel

For thick and heavy floor or wall tile, over twelve inches: Half-inch square-notched or U-shaped trowel

Planning the Layout

This step is a big one, as it directly effects the visual aesthetics of your installation. Whether you're tiling a floor, countertop, backsplash, or

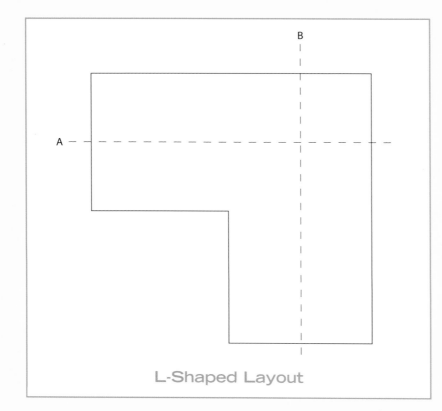

B

A

L-Shaped Layout

Diagonal layouts. To arrive at a diagonal pattern, refer back to your original perpendicular working lines. From these intersecting lines, create another set of lines by measuring out from the center point along each of the four legs any given distance and making a mark. Use the 3-4-5 triangle method to draw a line perpendicular to the original reference line, and repeat this process on all four legs, thus creating a square. The diagonal lines between the intersecting corners should equal 45 degrees. Snap your chalk line between the diagonal corners and use these new lines to guide your diagonal layout.

L-shaped rooms. When you're planning to tile an L-shaped room, you treat it as you would any other room by graphing your layout and making adjustments on paper, then checking walls for square. It is important to consider the entire expanse as a whole, not as two separate entities. Snap intersecting reference lines, one in each leg of the L. If possible, create your grid system by marking lines from the longest wall in each area of the L-shaped room. Be sure to locate the focal points in each area, and pay particular attention to these, avoiding cuts here if at all possible.

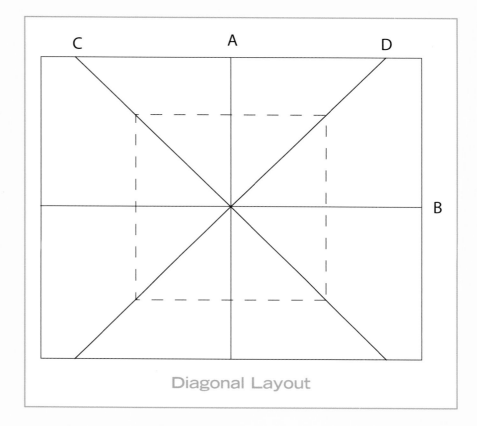

C   A   D

B

Diagonal Layout

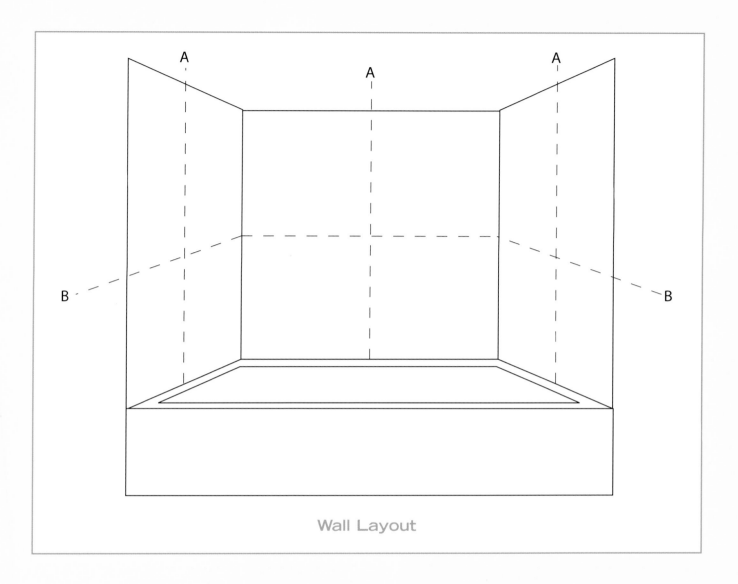

Wall Layout

Wall layouts. As you did with the flooring layout, create a scale drawing of the area to be tiled on graph paper. With tracing paper and colored pencils, experiment to discover the best design for your space. Make adjustments to allow for full tiles (or at minimum, symmetrical cuts greater than half a tile) at primary focal points, such as prominent architectural features, a niche, a vent hood and range combination, or a window in the shower. When tiling walls without a major focal feature, it is best to center tiles, allowing for balanced cuts at either end. When planning an intricate wall design (a backsplash or shower wall, for example), sketch the layout to full scale on the wall that will actually be receiving the tile, marking either directly on the surface or on kraft paper that has been taped in place. Step back, and you will notice right away if adjustments need to be made. In showers, plan for equal cuts to fall around focal points such as plumbing and niches. Before setting any tile, check the walls for plumb and square using a level. Flat and plumb surfaces on vertical tile applications are very important, as these areas are in direct line with the visual plane,

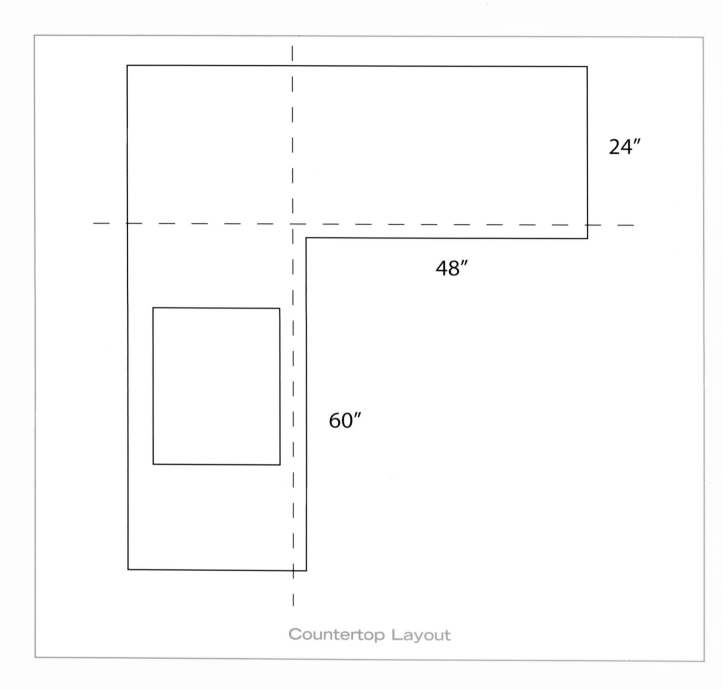

24"

48"

60"

Countertop Layout

and mistakes or tapered cuts are difficult to disguise. You may remedy problems by floating out skewed walls with mortar to create a true plane. Just before you set your tile, snap horizontal and vertical reference lines with chalk as you would on a floor (you can also mark these lines using a straightedge and pencil). Double-check these perpendicular lines for square. Finally, dry-fit the actual tile that will placed on the wall and adjust the layout in real time, using a batten board if necessary. This is the best way to ensure symmetrical cuts at all corners and focal points.

Countertop layouts. Because countertops are small horizontal areas at waist level, they are one of the easier layouts to configure. In fact, the best way to formulate the ideal plan is through dry-fitting the actual tiles you plan to use on the countertop surface itself. In real time, you can move them one way or another to create symmetrical cuts around focal points such as the sink or stove. Reference lines are helpful for marking exactly where you want your tile and sink rail to fall, especially after you have removed the tiles from the counter in preparation for setting them. The most important aspect of countertop design is ensuring that full tiles are placed at the front edge, and cut tiles fall at the back, where they will be disguised somewhat by the backsplash. If you are tiling an L-shaped countertop, it may be best to start with a full set of tiles at the intersection of the legs of the L and work out from there. Of particular importance are flat and level substrates upon which to tile, with enough height to offer room for an adequate edge profile. In addition, consider keeping grout joints narrow on a tiled countertop, leaving less room for debris to collect.

Setting the Tile

This is the part you have been waiting for! All of the research, planning, and prep work has now brought you to the point of actually tiling. Although you will become familiar with more in-depth tile-setting information in the next three chapters, a few rules apply to just about every job.

Before you get to work, make sure you have all of your setting material and tools on the job site and ready to go. There is no bigger pain than realizing that a crucial item is missing only when you are on your knees with a batch of freshly mixed mortar at your side. Even worse is finding that you are running short on tile when you're most of the way through a job. To avoid these frustrations, double-check that everything you need to set the tile is close at hand, and that you have checked your tile order carefully for correct color, shading, amount, and any breakage before you get started.

Next, be sure that your working area is clean and organized. By now you will have gone through the boxes or crates of tile and observed any irregularities in color and shading. To arrive at the most attractive installation, blend together tiles from all containers to avoid obvious patches of dark or light color. Making stacks of dark, medium, and light helps to ensure proper blending. As you prepare your space for tiling, make small stacks of tile within arm's reach so that you do not have to get up every few minutes for another tile. Work in the small grids that you marked with chalk earlier, completing each one before you move to the next.

As you go along setting your tile, be sure to check frequently that your installation remains square and level. Clean any thinset that may squeeze up between tiles with a damp sponge as you work, and maintain an organized work zone. As you place each tile in the setting material, press or lightly twist it into the mortar to ensure proper coverage. You may also use a rubber mallet to tap tiles into place. As you continue to work, pull up a tile periodically to check that the thinset adequately covers its backside.

Depending on your particular situation, you may want to precut tiles, or you may prefer to make cuts as you go. This is where having a tile buddy comes in handy. If cuts fall in highly visible areas, it is best to wait until you get to that point to cut them for the most accurate fit and best look.

After your space has been tiled, be sure to mark it off so that no one walks on it for at least twenty-four hours. It is also a good idea, when working in new construction, to protect your installation from damage with kraft paper or cardboard.

Grouting the Tile

Grout serves several purposes in a tile installation with regard to both form and function. It increases the integrity of the entire installation and prevents dirt from accumulating in the spaces between the tiles. Grout also reduces the amount of water that can make its way below the tile, while providing the finishing aesthetic touch. Grout is a necessary part of any tiling job, even if it is not one of the most pleasurable.

In general terms, grout is a colored mortar composed primarily of Portland cement, available in premixed and dry powder form. Both sanded and nonsanded grouts are available. Nonsanded grout is commonly used in joints smaller than an eighth of an inch, or in conjunction with delicate tiles and polished stones that may scratch. Sanded grout is used in joints of one-eighth inch or larger, or where added strength is required. Another choice, epoxy grout, is commonly associated with commercial installations, as it is a superior product that maintains its color, does not stain, and is resistant to chemicals. However, working with epoxy is somewhat akin to working with tar, and therein lies the tradeoff.

Manufacturers have done their best to develop products that alleviate many of the problems once associated with grout. New types are commonly fortified with polymers that add strength and flexibility (to prevent cracking), inhibit mold and mildew growth, and maintain even color. Upcoming chapters will go into more depth on the correct preparation and application of grout in specific installations; here we will discuss the most common evils associated with grout, to help you avoid them.

Cracking. One of the most common complaints with regard to grout is cracking, which can result from a variety of factors. For example, the grout used may be too old, or it may not have been mixed according to the manufacturer's directions (using too much water weakens grout). It may be that the installer did not pack the joints well enough, or that too much setting material rose up between the joints (grout should fill two-thirds of the joint space). Perhaps expansion joints were filled with grout instead of flexible caulk. Sometimes the problem is related not to the grout itself, but to the substrate below. If movement in the substrate telegraphs to the tile installation above, grout may crack.

Discoloration. This is another big problem. Because grout contributes greatly to the look of the finished installation, mottling or variation in color can result in quite an eyesore. Discoloration occurs for several reasons. Most commonly the grout is mixed with either too much or too little water or is not allowed time to slake after mixing. In addition, each batch may have used a different ratio of powder to water. It is extremely important to use the same mixture each and every time to ensure an exact color match. Another problem that causes discoloration is the use of too much water when cleaning grout residue and haze. This can dilute pigments, resulting in uneven color. If setting material has risen too high between the joints, one area may appear lighter or darker than another. A commonly overlooked issue that can lead to color imbalance is the overglazing of tile. This results in water being wicked from the grout at different rates, which may cause shade variations. Lastly, the use of harsh cleaning agents such as ammonia or bleach will surely discolor grout. Use a neutral-pH cleaner instead. Once your grout has cured for approximately seventy-two hours and is immaculately clean, be sure to apply a penetrating sealer to ensure easy care and long-lasting beauty.

Irregularities. In addition to cracking and discoloration, general irregularities can damage the overall aesthetics of the tile installation. Problems arise when grout varies in depth from one area to the next. Some joints may be flush and some recessed, when ideally they should all be smooth and even. A cheap or dirty grout float can create nicks, holes, and scratches. Be sure to spend the extra money on a sharp, clean float. Lastly, grout joints may look irregular because the setter did not space precisely. Taking the time to align joints, using spacers, and setting tile carefully will ensure that grout joints appear perfect in the end.

Haze. Last but certainly not least, grout haze is a frequent source of complaint. If you are working with a porous tile, such as limestone or terra-cotta, be sure to seal the tile well with a penetrating sealer first. Next, try to remove as much excess grout as you can during the actual process by using the grout float as a squeegee, holding it at a 90-degree angle to the tile. Many try to clean up grout too fast with too much water. The key is to allow it to firm in the joints slightly (over ten to twenty minutes or so), then wipe with a clean, damp sponge diagonally to the joints. Wipe, flip the sponge, wipe again, then rinse. Have clean water on hand at all times so you do not reapply the haze. After the majority of the grout has been cleaned from the tile surface, use a clean, dry cloth to buff away the powdery haze that continues to appear. Never let grout dry completely on the surface of your tile, and never apply a sealer to a tile surface that still has a layer of grout haze. After you have grouted, go back and fill expansion joints with flexible caulk, either standard, or sanded/nonsanded grout color-matched to the type found throughout the rest of your project.

Sealing the Tile

Sealers are used in conjunction with porous materials, such as grout, natural stone, terra-cotta, and unglazed tile, either to lock out moisture and stains or to enhance the tile's color. The most commonly used type of sealer is penetrating sealer, also known as impregnating sealer. Penetrating sealers may be water- or solvent-based and come in a variety of strengths. Some types may be inexpensive and last merely a year before another application is needed, while some come with a lifetime guarantee, thus rarely, if ever, requiring reapplication. This type of sealer soaks into the body of the tile, protecting it from moisture and stains from the inside out, and does not affect the surface appearance of the tile. In some cases, you may want to deepen the color of your tile, such as tumbled marble or slate; for this you will likely consider a topcoat sealer or color enhancer.

Depending on the manufacturer, this type of sealer may simply darken the color of the tile (offering a wet look) or provide a combination of protection and color enhancement. When choosing this type of sealer, be aware that it is offered in matte, satin, and glossy finishes. For the most natural effect, be sure to choose the matte. When applying a topcoat sealer, keep in mind that care should be taken during the application process not to leave swirl marks or streaks, as this will become very noticeable. In addition, it is important to know that topcoat sealers such as this, particularly on smooth surfaces such as travertine, limestone, and honed marble, can scratch and require occasional stripping and reapplication to look its best.

Finishing Up

After all of the planning, prep work, tile setting, grouting, caulking, and sealing has come to an end, it is time to finish up. If this is new construction, and more tradesmen will continue to work around your tile, protect it with kraft paper or cardboard taped in place. If the job is complete, go back and replace baseboards and/or shoe molding, adjust the height of doors as you replace them, and complete any outstanding details. Whew!

Material	Characteristics	Ideal Substrate	Setting Methods and Materials	Care
Brick	Bricks intended for flooring, at approximately 8x4x½ inches in size, are thinner than construction brick. They may be flat and smooth or rough and tumbled in appearance. Colors normally reflect the clay used in their creation, or can be altered through the addition of various pigments.	To install brick as flooring, the substrate must be strong, rigid, flat, and clean. Preferred underlayments consist of concrete or 1 to 2 layers of ¾-inch plywood with a final layer of ½-inch cement backer board.	Cut brick tile using a wet saw, an angle grinder fitted with a diamond/masonry blade, or a circular saw fitted with a masonry blade. Set with gray thinset and a ½-inch square-notched trowel. A ⅜-inch grout joint is often the norm. Seal brick prior to grouting.	Brick is porous and should be sealed well with a penetrating sealer before and after grouting. Sweep, vacuum, and mop with a neutral-pH cleaner as needed.
Glazed Floor Tiles	Glazed floor tiles are most commonly dust-pressed red body, vitreous or semi-vitreous monocottura tiles. Available in many colors, textures, sizes, and shapes, their thickness ranges from ⅜ to ¾-inch.	Substrates must be sturdy, rigid, flat, and clean. Tile can be set over existing floors in excellent shape; the preferred substrate, however, consists of concrete or a ¾-inch plywood and ½-inch cement backer board combination. Tiles can be used on walls as well.	Cuts can be made using a snap cutter, an angle grinder fitted with a diamond/masonry blade, or a wet saw. Use a square-notched trowel matched to the thickness of the tile and modified thinset in gray to set the tiles.	Glazed floor tile itself does not require sealing; however, it is wise to seal the grout. To clean simply sweep, vacuum, and mop as needed.
Glazed Wall Tiles	Glazed wall tiles are most commonly non-vitreous, white-bodied, dust-pressed tiles. Lighter, thinner, and softer than floor tiles, they are easily cut, shaped, and set into place. A wide variety of sizes, shapes, and colors are manufactured as well as numerous accents and finishing trims. Not intended for use on floors or countertops.	Suitable wall substrates located in dry locations can be comprised of drywall, greenboard, plaster, or plywood and should be intact, flat, and clean. In wet locations, such as showers, the substrate must be concrete backer board or a special membrane such as Kerdi.	Straight cuts can be made with a snap cutter, while odd cuts are best accomplished with tile nippers. Tile can also be cut using an angle grinder or wet saw. Install using the appropriate organic mastic in dry areas, or modified gray thinset using a ¼-inch V-notched trowel in wet areas.	There is no need to seal glazed wall tile, but sealing the grout is recommended. Use a gentle cleaning agent and soft rag to maintain.

Material	Characteristics	Ideal Substrate	Setting Methods and Materials	Care
Concrete	Concrete tile is either extruded or poured into molds and is dried rather than fired. Available in a wide variety of sizes, shapes, colors, textures, and finishes.	Ideal flooring substrates are concrete slab or one or two layers of ¾-inch plywood and ½-inch concrete backer board combination.	Cuts are best made with a wet saw, but an angle grinder fitted with a diamond/masonry blade or a circular saw with a masonry blade can also be used. Set with gray thinset, using a square-notched trowel that corresponds to the thickness of the tile. Seal the surface prior to grouting.	Concrete tiles are porous and should be sealed with a penetrating sealer. Clean by sweeping, vacuuming, and mopping with a neutral-pH cleaner as needed. Concrete acquires a unique patina as it ages.
Cork	Cork tile is cut from sheets into a variety of sizes and shapes, including squares, rectangles, and planks, and can be found stained a wide range of colors. Cork is soft, quiet, and comfortable underfoot and can be used on walls and ceilings as well.	Subfloors should be either well cured concrete or plywood and must be clean, dry, and flat. Irregularities and bumps on the substrate's surface will telegraph through the tile.	Acclimate the material on-site for several days prior to installation. Make cuts using a utility knife and straightedge. Tile is installed using the manufacturer's recommended adhesive.	Tile should be sealed with urethane according to manufacturer's directions. To maintain, simply sweep, vacuum, and damp-mop as needed. Over time, cork will acquire a leatherlike patina.
Glass	Glass is an impervious tile that is moisture- and stain-proof . It is found in a wide array of colors, sizes, shapes, textures, and finishes. Glass can be used for floors, walls, and countertops.	Flooring substrates should be either concrete or a plywood and cement board combination. In dry areas, walls can be drywall, plaster, masonry, or any clean, dry, stable surface.	Cut using a wet saw fitted with a glass-cutting blade. Set tiles using a ¼-inch **V**-notched trowel and white modified thinset. Clear glass must be set with flattened trowel marks, whereas opaque glass may be set with the notch marks left raised. Take care when installing mosaics to prevent setting material from squeezing up between the joints.	There is no need to seal glass tile, however, sealing the grout is recommended. Clean with a glass cleaner as needed, and buff with a soft, dry rag.

Material	Characteristics	Ideal Substrate	Setting Methods and Materials	Care
Leather	Leather tiles are available in a wide range of sizes, shapes, colors, textures, and finishes. Tiles are soft, supple, warm, and quiet.	Ideal subfloors are plywood or well-cured dry concrete.	Allow tile to acclimate at the job site for 48 hours prior to setting. Blend tiles from all boxes to ensure even color flow. Cut with a utility knife and straightedge. Set tiles tightly, using the manufacturer's recommended adhesive.	Once set, treat leather tiles with several coatings of carnauba wax, buffing between each coat with a soft, dry rag. Sweep and spot-clean with a damp rag as needed. Leather will acquire a beautiful patina over the years with use.
Linoleum	Linoleum tiles are made from all-natural materials. Soft and resilient, tiles are commonly available 12 to 18-inches square and in numerous colors, textures, and surface patterns.	Ideal subfloors include intact resilient flooring, plywood, and well-cured dry concrete. Subfloor must be dry, clean, and absolutely flat. Any bumps or irregularities will show through the tile's surface.	Allow tiles to acclimate on the job site for a minimum of 48 hours. Blend material from all boxes to ensure even color flow. Cut tiles using a utility knife and straightedge. Set tiles tightly, using the manufacturer's recommended adhesive.	No need to seal tiles. Simply sweep, vacuum, and damp-mop with a neutral-pH cleaner as needed. Over time, linoleum actually becomes stronger as the linseed oil it is created from matures.
Stone	Natural stone tiles are cut from blocks excavated from the earth and include granite, marble, travertine, slate, limestone, and soapstone, among others. Available in a vast array of sizes, thicknesses, shapes, colors, textures, and finishes.	Substrates must be able to bear a heavy load and be rigid, clean, dry, and flat. Concrete or one or two layers of ¾-inch plywood and ½-inch cement backer board combination are best for floors. Walls in dry areas can be drywall, greenboard, masonry, or plaster in excellent condition.	Blend tiles from all crates to ensure good color flow. Cut using a diamond-blade wet saw or a diamond-blade angle grinder. Light-colored tiles should be set with a white modified thinset or marble and granite mix, using a trowel that corresponds to the thickness of the tile. Dark-colored tiles can be set using a gray modified thinset. Seal tiles before grouting.	Natural stone tiles are porous and should be sealed with a penetrating sealer. Clean by sweeping, vacuuming, and mopping with a neutral-pH cleaner as needed. Nearly all unpolished stones improve in appearance with age and use.

Material	Characteristics	Ideal Substrate	Setting Methods and Materials	Care
Parquet	Tiles are created using small pieces of wood joined to create a larger geometric pattern. Numerous sizes, colors, and patterns available.	Ideal substrates include plywood and well-cured dry concrete.	Allow parquet tiles to acclimate on the job site for 24 hours. Blend from all containers to ensure even color flow. Most parquet tile is either nail-down or glue-down tongue-and-groove. Make cuts using a circular saw or jigsaw. Use the manufacturer's recommended adhesive to set.	Evaluate need for refinishing over the years. Sweep or vacuum tiles to remove dust and dirt. Damp-mop with a wood cleaner as needed. Natural and artificial light exposure will cause wood to change in color over time. Keep this in mind when using area rugs.
Porcelain	Porcelain is a dust-pressed white clay tile that is high-fired to form a vitreous or impervious body. Can be glazed or unglazed. Enormous range of sizes, shapes, colors, textures, and finishes available. Popular look-alikes include stone, wood, textiles, terra-cotta, and metal.	Ideal substrates include concrete or a ¾-inch plywood and cement backer board combination. Wall tiles in dry areas can be set over any clean, durable, flat, and intact substrate.	Cut tiles using a diamond-blade wet saw. Set in place with a modified thinset mortar with a square-notched trowel corresponding in thickness to the tile.	Unglazed porcelain tiles must be sealed prior to grouting and to prevent staining. To clean, simply sweep, vacuum, and mop as needed.
Metal	Solid metal is impervious to stains and moisture. Some tiles are created from real metal such as bronze, brass, aluminum, steel, iron, copper, and nickel, whereas some are ceramic and resin bodies coated with liquid metal. Wide variety of options available in size, shape, texture, and finish, as well as decorative accents and borders.	Ideal flooring substrates are concrete and plywood dressed with cement backer board. Walls in dry locations can be drywall, greenboard, plaster, masonry, or any clean, dry, intact surface.	Cut tiles using a hacksaw, or an angle grinder fitted with a metal cutting blade. Metal coated tiles can be cut using a wet saw. Roughen the backsides of solid metal tiles with sandpaper to improve adhesion. Setting material should be modified thinset in gray or, if metal tiles are used as an accent, whatever setting material is being employed for the remainder of the tile.	Clean tiles with a soft, dry rag. Solid metal tiles will acquire a patina over time and can be buffed back to new with a metal cleaner. A small amount of paste wax will delay the aging process.

Material	Characteristics	Ideal Substrate	Setting Methods and Materials	Care
Mosaic	Ceramic and porcelain mosaics are 2 inches or less in size and are available in numerous configurations, including netted sheets of hexagons, pennies, chicklets, random patterns, and squares.	Substrates should be concrete or a plywood and cement backer board combination. Floors and walls should be flat, as any imperfections will show under the tiny tiles.	Cut using a snap cutter, tile nipper, or wet saw. Install mosaic with a small ¼-inch **V**-notched trowel and a thinset that closely matches the color of the grout you intended to use, as some setting material inevitably squeezes up between the joints. Seal unglazed porcelain prior to grouting.	To clean, sweep, vacuum, or mop with a gentle cleaner.
Quarry	Quarry tile is extruded and semivitreous or vitreous in nature. Common thickness falls between ½-inch and ¾-inches, with sizes ranging from 3- to 12-inch squares and 3x6- and 4x8-inch rectangles to standard hexagons. Color reflects the clay used to form the tile and is the same top to bottom. Normally sold unglazed.	Ideal substrates are concrete or one or two layers of ¾-inch plywood covered with a layer of ½-inch cement backer board. Substrate should be clean, flat, and strong.	Cut tiles with a wet saw or diamond/masonry blade angle grinder. Set with gray modified thinset using a ½-inch to ¾-inch square-notched trowel. Seal prior to grouting.	Once the grout has cured (48 hours), seal the tile's surface again with a penetrating sealer. Sweep, vacuum, and mop with a neutral-pH cleaner as needed.
Rubber	Rubber tiles are very durable as well as soft, warm, quiet, and comfortable underfoot. Tiles come in a variety of fun colors and embossed patterns in sizes ranging from 12x12- to 48x48-inch squares.	Tile must be installed over a clean, dry, flat subfloor, preferably of plywood or concrete.	Allow tiles to acclimate a minimum of 24 hours in the space where they will be installed. Cut with a utility knife and straightedge and set with manufacturer's recommended epoxy adhesive.	Rubber tiles are tough, but may stain with oil and grease. Refer to manufacturer's directions to learn if your particular tile must be sealed. Clean by sweeping, vacuuming, and damp-mopping with a gentle cleaner as needed.

Material	Characteristics	Ideal Substrate	Setting Methods and Materials	Care
Terra Cotta	Terra-cotta is a nonvitreous clay tile that is soft and porous in nature. The color of the tile runs true top to bottom and reflects the color of the clay used in its creation. A variety of shades, sizes, shapes, textures, and finishes are available.	Ideal substrates include concrete or a plywood and cement backer board combination. Substrate should be clean, flat, strong, rigid, and free from defects.	Blend tiles from all containers to ensure a pleasing color flow. Cut using a wet saw or angle grinder fitted with a diamond/masonry blade. Set using gray modified thinset. Seal prior to grouting.	Once grout has cured, seal the surface again with a penetrating sealer. Clean by sweeping, vacuuming, or mopping with a gentle cleanser.
Vinyl	Soft, quiet, durable tile made from synthetic materials. Tiles may be glue-down or peel-and-stick. Available in a wide variety of colors and surface patterns. Tiles often mimic other materials such as mosaic, ceramic, stone, brick, and wood.	Vinyl tiles can be placed over existing floor tile if it is clean, flat, and intact. Ideally the floor should be plywood or well-cured concrete.	Allow tiles to acclimate in their intended location for 24 hours. Cut with a vinyl cutter or utility knife and straightedge. Set glue-down tiles with manufacturer's recommended adhesive.	Sweep, vacuum, and clean with a gentle no-rinse cleaner as needed. Direct sunlight may cause vinyl tile to yellow over time.

chapter 9 | in the kitchen

Although it has been said many times before, the notion remains true—the kitchen is the heart of the home. The core around which the entire house revolves, this all-inclusive space is an integral part of our daily lives. Here, we nourish our body, mind, and spirit through the cooking of meals, stolen moments alone with a hot cup of coffee and the morning newspaper, and evenings spent musing over old photographs with a dear friend. This space must be efficient, hygienic, durable, stylish, and func-tional. With so much riding on kitchen style and function, materials that offer both strength and beauty are imperative. Tile in the kitchen must hold its own against a daily assault of hot pots and pans, a variety of cooking activities and utensils, a laundry list of liq-uids, and extremely heavy traffic. In this chapter, we've selected granite, glass, and metal as the funda-mental ingredients of our design. All of these elements offer the traits necessary to be both practical and attractive. You may choose to make changes in tile

granite tile countertop with a glass and metal backsplash

Estimated time to install: Five days, with a helper

Skill level: Advanced, with general tile-setting skills

Materials

- Granite tiles with laminated bullnose edge; color, Imperial Sage
- Clear glass mosaic tile, one inch square; color, Fern
- White bronze tiles, three by three inches; style, Lotus
- Black nonsanded grout (Hydroment) for countertop
- Avocado green sanded grout (Hydroment) for backsplash

- Sanded caulk to match backsplash
- Five-eighths-inch plywood
- One-quarter inch cement backer board
- Latex-modified thinset
- Galvanized screws
- Drill
- Fiberglass mesh tape
- Grease pen
- Wrench
- Screwdriver
- Hacksaw
- Level

- Wedges or cardboard shims
- Pry bar
- Hammer
- Measuring tape
- Carpenter's pencil and sharpener
- Carpenter's square
- Circular saw
- Wet saw
- Margin trowel
- Three-sixteenths inch V-notched trowel
- One-quarter by one-quarter inch square-notched trowel

- Angle grinder with diamond blade
- Utility knife
- Graph paper
- Kraft paper
- Tape
- Stone sealer
- Spray bottle
- Clean cloth
- Buckets
- Sponges
- Grout float
- Grout sealer applicator

color, size, shape, or texture, or you may follow the project to the letter. Either way, the end result will be a charming new kitchen, ready to be filled with life, laughter, and love.

The Countertop

Step 1: Evaluate your space, plan your layout, and gather materials. One of the most important components of a tile project is planning. This includes predetermining what tiles you want to use, and where; how many square feet you will need; and what tools you must rent, buy, or borrow to get the project done. If you're remodeling, how long will the space be out of commission? And finally, you must sort through the details of the actual installation itself.

Drawing the space to be tiled to scale on a sheet of graph paper will help you discover the ideal design and layout. Initial adjustments are much easier to make on paper than with real tiles. Fine-tune the tile spacing to eliminate cuts smaller than half a tile. Consider major focal points in your design, such as the sink, stove, or a window, and manipulate your layout to allow tiles to fall symmetrically around them. Walk through the project step by step on paper, listing everything you need and creating, in a sense, a project planner. Having all the tools and materials on hand and in good repair when the project commences will make life much easier and allow the installation to progress smoothly.

Step 2: Get the space ready to tile. If you are remodeling, plan to do some demolition. Depending on the scope of your project, this might involve simply removing a countertop, sink,

and a few old tiles, or it might mean ripping the entire place apart, cabinets, appliances, flooring, and all. In general, to remove items from a kitchen, you need safety equipment, such as eye protection, ear protection, and a dust mask, and simple tools, including a pry bar, a hammer, a floor/wall scraper, and a utility knife. To remove the kitchen sink, you need to shut off the water, place a bucket under the plumbing to catch any overflow, and use a wrench to loosen pipes. A utility knife can loosen caulk where the countertop meets the wall, and a pry bar helps lift it from its position. Getting everything out of the way and cleaning things up allows you to better visualize your project. Now you are on your way.

Step 3: Prepare the substrate and make cutouts. Once the old countertop and backsplash have been removed, inspect your cabinets to make sure they are plumb and level. Make adjustments as needed. Walls behind cabinets that are out of square will cause problems when setting the countertop tile; plan to adjust your cuts accordingly. Most importantly, tiles must be straight along the front edge.

Now it is time to prepare the substrate for your tile—the plywood and cement board.

Plywood

Measure the top of the cabinets and transfer these measurements onto your sheet of five-eighths-inch plywood (the thickness recommended with laminated bullnose granite tiles). Allow the front edge of the plywood to fall flush with the front edge of your cabinets. Cut the plywood to the correct size with a circular saw. Once it has been cut, place the plywood on the counter and trace the sink (follow the manufacturer's directions); our sink required us to trace a line one-quarter inch inside the outer perimeter. Take the plywood back off the countertop and cut out the sink hole using a circular saw. Next, screw the plywood to the cabinetry from the underside, making sure that it is rigid and securely in place.

Cement Board

Lay the uncut sheet of cement board on top of your plywood, once it is secured in place. With your pencil, scribe a line along the underside of the cement board, using the plywood as a guide. Cut along this line with an angle grinder outfitted with a diamond blade, or with your circular saw. To mark the sink, place the cut piece of cement board over the plywood and, from underneath, trace the existing sink cutout. Using your angle grinder or circular saw, make your sink cutout. To attach the cement board to the plywood, you must use both thinset and screws. Using a margin trowel, mix the dry thinset with water in a bucket, to a consistency similar to toothpaste or cake frosting. Using the flat side of the trowel, place a few scoops of thinset on the plywood. Spread the thinset using the **V**-notched side of the trowel. Continue to add and spread thinset until even coverage has been obtained. Place the cement board over the plywood, then secure in place with the manufacturer's recommended fasteners (normally galvanized screws). Place the screws at intervals of six inches at the perimeter, and eight inches in the field. Be sure to countersink all screw heads. Cover the cement board seams with thinset and fiberglass mesh tape. Clean the substrate with a damp sponge, and get ready to tile.

Step 4: Set the tile. Here is where your early planning comes in handy. Pull out your graph paper and dry-fit the countertop tiles according to your drawing. Make any final adjustments to the layout.

Following your dry layout, measure and mark the required cuts. Marking the line with a grease pen will help prevent it from being washed away. With a diamond-blade wet saw, cut your tile slowly along the line by easing it away from you, through the blade. Do not force the tile. After each cut, place the tile in its intended location and review how the design is coming together. Once all of the tiles are cut and dry-fit, and you are pleased with the configuration, it is time to set the tiles.

Set the tiles aside. Keep track of where each tile came from; if necessary, label the underside. Use white thinset marble and granite mix to lay your stone tiles, mixing to the consistency of icing. Using a quarter inch square-notched trowel, spread the thinset as you did with the plywood and cement board. Once you have an even coverage of mortar over a workable area—about four feet—pick up the first tile and back-butter it to ensure adequate adhesion. Starting with the front corner edge, set the tile in place. Next, set the tile behind it. As you move along, be sure to back-butter each tile, and check often that the tiles are level. With a damp sponge, clean any thinset that may be adhering to tile edges or squeezing up between them. Also, make sure that each drawer front comfortably opens underneath the tiles as you go. As you set each consecutive tile, run your finger along the grout joint to determine if the tiles are even. If you notice lippage (one tile edge sits higher than the next), remove the tile and either add or subtract thinset in the problem area until it is smooth and even. Check the front edge of the countertop with a level to ensure the tiles are straight. Continue this sequence, back-buttering and checking for level and lippage, until you are done. Allow the tiles to set up overnight before you move on to the next step.

Step 5: Grout the tile. Tightly set granite tile requires a nonsanded grout. Before grouting, seal the granite tile with a penetrating sealer made for natural stone (available at local home centers).

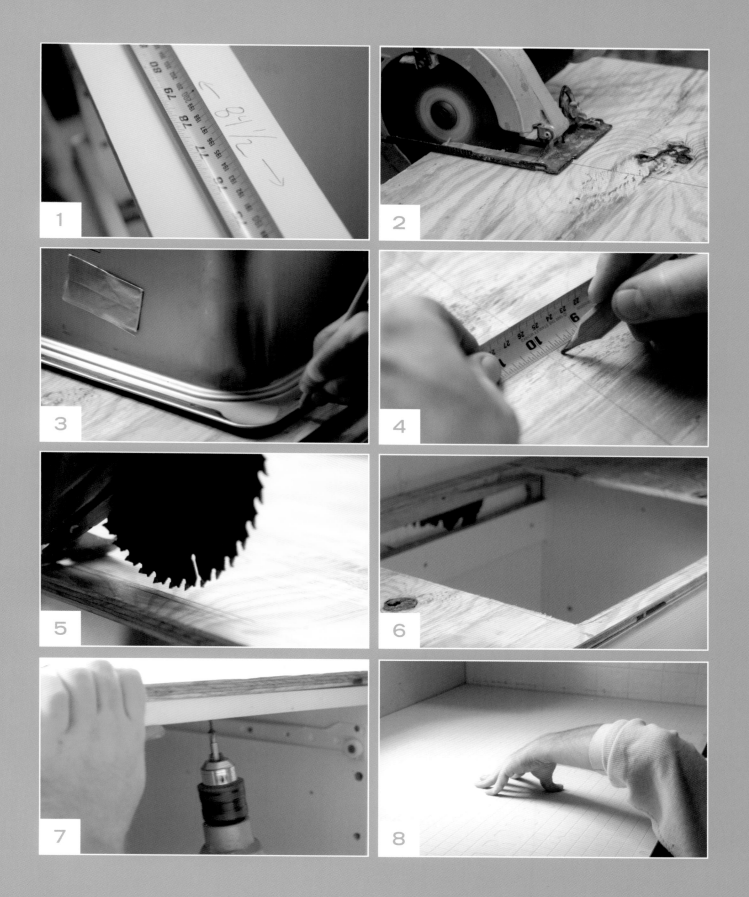

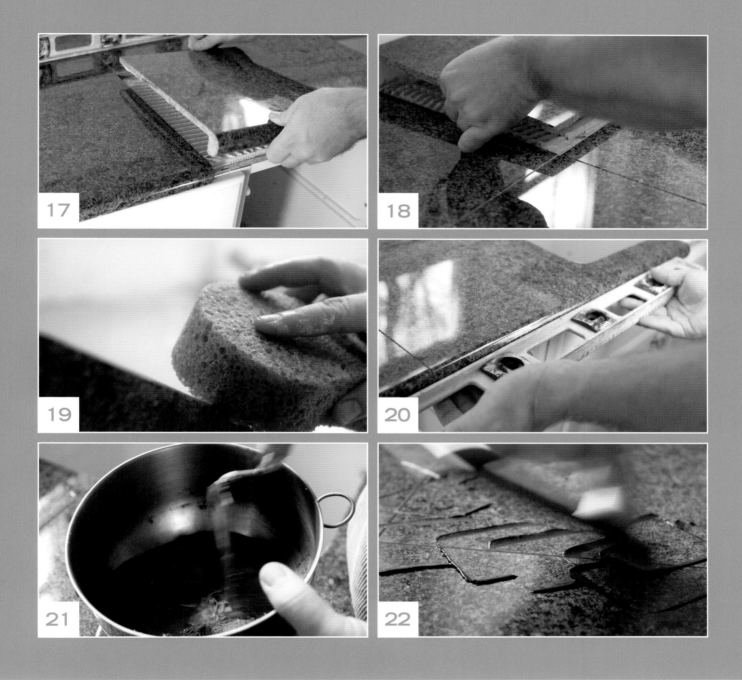

With a spray bottle, spritz on an even coat of sealer, allow a moment for it to soak in, and then wipe the excess away with a clean rag. Apply only one coat at this point; after the grout has had time to cure, you will perform the final sealing. Tape off the backsplash tile if it has already been installed.

When the area to be grouted is very small, mix the grout in a small container rather than a big bucket. Adhering to the manufacturer's directions, use a margin trowel to mix the powdered grout with water to a smooth consistency, similar to creamy peanut butter. Allow approximately ten minutes for the grout to slake. With the margin trowel, dab a few scoops of grout onto the countertop. Use a grout float to press the grout firmly into the joints at a 45-degree angle. Go back and forth over each joint until it is full and flush. Use the side of the grout float to remove excess grout from the tile surface. Allow time for the grout to set up slightly (ten minutes or so), and then, with a damp sponge, begin to remove the excess grout, or haze, from the tile surface. Clean across the joints at a 45-degree angle. Be careful not to remove grout from the joints, and do not introduce too much water, or the grout may exhibit efflorescence (a white chalky appearance). Once the initial cleanup is complete and the grout has had time to set up sufficiently, go back over the tiles once again with a soft, dry towel to buff them to a brilliant shine. Allow the grout forty-eight hours to cure, and then seal it well.

Step 6: Seal the tile. The final task before the countertop is complete is to seal the stone and grout together. Make sure the countertop is clean. Apply a liberal amount of sealer, allowing it time to penetrate both the grout and tile. If all of the sealer soaks in rather quickly, wait a moment and apply another coat until it will no longer accept the sealer. Remove any remaining sealer with a rag. Allow time for the surface to dry (about an hour or two). Then replace your sink, and start using your kitchen again!

The Backsplash

Step 1: Plan. The backsplash is quite literally one of the first things you notice when you enter a kitchen. It should be beautiful, symmetrical, and pull the entire room together. The planning stage is very important; as with the countertop, it is important to draw your design to scale on graph paper. Determine ahead of time where to place cuts so that they are equal, especially around focal points. In our project, we had a window to contend with in an older home, where absolutely nothing was square nor centered,

so we needed to finesse our design here and there. In addition, glass tile can be difficult to work with, but if you prepare well and know the proper steps to take, things will go smoothly.

Step 2: Prepare the wall. Ensure that the wall where you will install the glass tile is clean, flat, and smooth. To achieve this, remove all old tile or wallpaper—whatever existed there before. Scrape the surface to remove ridges, bumps, and old adhesive, filling any major defects with thinset or drywall mud. Knock down any high spots as well. Once you are satisfied with the substrate, it is time to get to work.

Step 3: Set the tile. Refer back to the layout you have drawn on graph paper. Dry-fit a few tiles (hold in place by hand) to double-check the accuracy of your drawing. If needed, draw the layout to full-size scale on the wall, as this will help you visualize the final outcome immensely. With glass mosaic, you must be absolutely precise in setting each sheet, or a grid pattern will show. Tape off your countertop with kraft paper, gather all of your tools and materials, and get ready to tile.

Because this design features heavy solid bronze liners and accents, it is important to work in small sections so the glass does not sag under the weight and squeeze the grout joints together. We decided that in our design, a row of three tiles high looked best, so we cut strips of three from the full-size netted sheets using a utility knife. To set the glass, use white modified thinset; mix it thicker than with the countertop tiles, to improve vertical adhesion. Use a small **V**-notched trowel to set the first row of tiles along the entire length of the splash. The particular glass chosen for our project has a frosted back, which affords us the luxury of not having to smooth the notches of the thinset. If you choose a clear glass tile, you must be sure the thinset is completely flat, with no ridges, or you will see them. When placing the first row of tile, use wedges or spacers to hold the tile slightly above the countertop (approximately one-

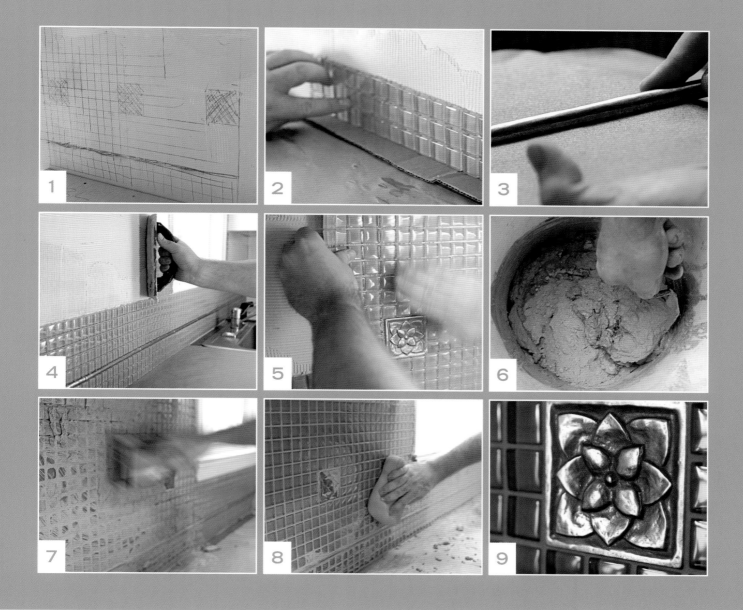

eighth of an inch). It is absolutely vital that the first row of mosaic be set straight and level. Use your carpenter's level as a guide. Scrutinize the tiles to ensure that the grout joints are even, and you do not notice where one strip meets the next. It should look like one continuous row of tile. Also, check that no setting material has pushed its way up through the tiles; if it has, it must be removed immediately, or it will cause headaches when you eventually grout. Allow the first row of tile to set up overnight before you move on to the rest of the design.

Day 2. Begin by setting the bronze bar liner on top of the first row of glass. Roughen the back of the metal with sandpaper, and make any cuts using a hacksaw. Set them in place with thinset. Next, plan exactly where your decorative bronze accents will go and tile all the way up to them. This will be your stopping point for today, as the

Before

new glass tiles must set up before you can install the heavy accent tiles. Once again, check that all of the mosaic sheets look like one continuous piece and adjust as necessary while the thinset is workable.

Day 3. Get ready to set the bronze accents. Double-check their placement, sand the backs, and set them in place with modified thinset. Once in place, surround them with the remainder of the glass tiles. Now it is time to start making cuts, if you haven't had to already. Cuts will be made at the outer edges of the installation, if need be, and around any obstacles, such as outlets or windows. Glass can be cut with a diamond-blade wet saw, or with a wet saw fitted with a special glass-cutting blade. The hard part is keeping the tiles from wiggling during the cutting process. One way to keep them from doing so is to tape the tiles where they need to be cut with blue painter's tape, which will keep shifting to a minimum. To fit small cuts in awkward places, use the margin trowel rather than

the V-notched trowel to spread the thinset. You can also back-butter individual tiles and pop them in here and there. Look the tiles over one last time to ensure that they appear continuous, and that there is no setting material in the grout joints. Allow the tiles to set up overnight in preparation for grouting.

Step 4: Grout the tiles. The larger joint spacing of these glass tiles requires a sanded grout. Be sure the countertop is covered well before grouting, and for ease of cleanup, tape the faces of decorative bronze tiles. Following the manufacturer's directions, use a margin trowel to mix the powdered grout to a smooth consistency with water. Allow approximately ten minutes for the grout to slake. With the grout float loaded with a sufficient amount of material, begin forcing it into the joints at a 45-degree angle. Go back and forth over each joint until it is full and flush. Use the side of the grout float to remove excess from the surface. In very tight spaces where the float will not fit, use your hands, protected with gloves, to grout the tile. Allow time for the grout to set up slightly (ten minutes or so) and, with a damp sponge, start to remove the excess grout and haze. Clean across the joints at a 45-degree angle. Be careful not to remove grout from the joints, and not to use an excessive amount of water. Once the initial cleanup is done and the grout has had time to set up further, go back over the tiles again with a soft, dry towel, buffing the glass to a glossy shine. Allow the grout forty-eight hours to cure, and then seal it well. Where the countertop meets the backsplash, fill the juncture with caulk, ideally in the same color as your backsplash grout.

Step 5: Seal the grout. Using a grout sealer and a special applicator made to fit just inside the joint, seal all of the grout joints. Tedious as this may be, it will keep the grout looking brand-new. Be sure to remove any excess sealer that may have gotten on the glass tiles with a soft cloth.

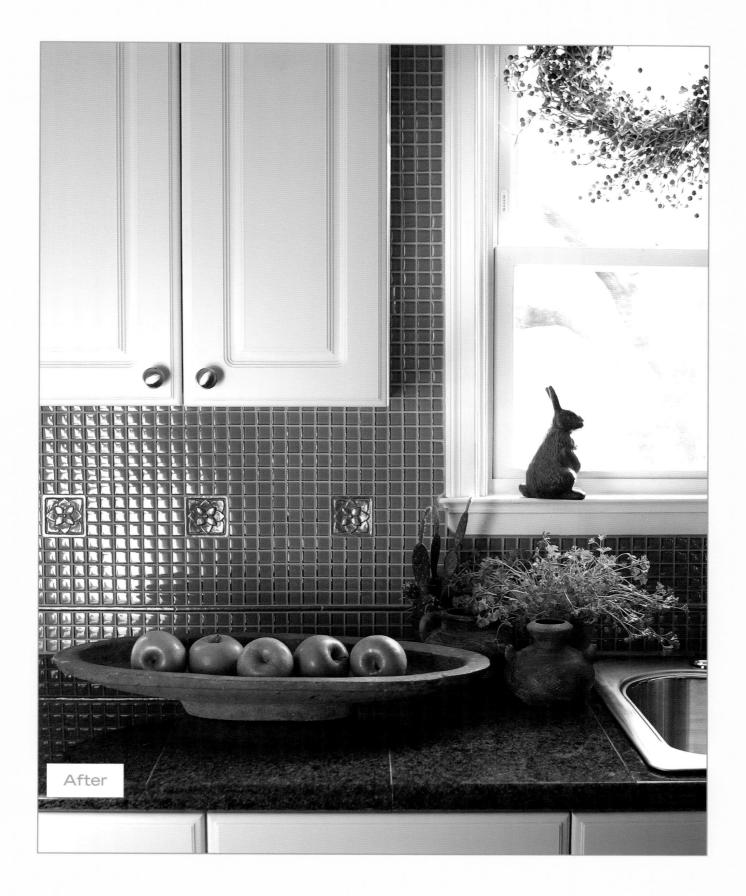

After

chapter 10 | **in the bath**

Once a claustrophobic, cold, and uninviting space in which we hurried through our daily routine, the outdated bath of the past has been treated to an extreme makeover and is now regarded as one of the most beautiful spaces within the home. Sprawling master bath retreats often rival those found at five-star resorts with their sublime surface detailing and grand amenities, including ample his and hers vanities, deep whirlpool tubs, and massive walk-in steam showers. No longer clad with standard-issue tile and mundane sheets of synthetic flooring, today's bathroom exudes an incomparable luxury and elegance with lush materials like creamy onyx, satin-smooth marble, and delicate handcrafted mosaics. With all of this extravagance just steps away, is it any wonder we continue to spend more and more of our free time at this bastion we call home?

Of course, not all of us have within our means the ability to tear down walls to erect such a ostentatious temple to bathing; we must work within the framework of our existing environment. Although your dreams may be full of images of the exquisite retreats found emblazoned across the covers of home design magazines, do not despair if the vision is currently out of reach. Simply revamping an outdated bath with a fresh coat of paint, crisp, clean tiles, sparkling new fixtures, and thoughtful decorative touches can work absolute wonders.

In this chapter, we focus on updating an older bath in need of a facelift. To achieve the best look for the existing style of the home and the small budget allotted, we chose a classic subway brick tile for the shower walls, paired with a one-inch hexagonal mosaic on the floor. This combination offers a timeless look at a reasonable cost, while maintaining ease of installation for the amateur tile setter.

While this project features an extremely popular tile combination, do not feel you must follow it to the letter. If your home decor requires a different style, color, or pattern of tile, go ahead and make the necessary changes, as the installation procedure is much the same. In the end, everything boils down to good planning and a thoughtful installation.

The Tub Surround

Step 1: Evaluate your space, plan your layout, and gather materials. Before you dive right into designing a bathroom, spend plenty

Materials

- Three-by-six-inch white semigloss tile (Daltile)
- One-inch-square black-and-white porcelain checkerboard mosaic (Daltile)
- Two-by-six-inch surface bullnose caps (Daltile)
- Two-by-six-inch or larger ceramic crown molding in white
- One-inch porcelain hexagonal mosaic in white (Daltile)

- Kerdi underlayment (Schlüter Systems)
- Kerdi band, if desired (Schlüter Systems)
- Ditra underlayment (Schlüter Systems)
- Nonsanded custom grout for floors and shower walls: color, Winter Gray
- Graph paper
- Pencil
- Utility knife
- Pry bar
- Hammer
- Chisel

- Wall/floor scraper
- Drop cloth
- Scissors
- Four-foot level
- Carpenter's square
- Measuring tape
- Wrench
- Screwdriver
- Wedges or shims
- Wet saw or score-and-snap tile cutter
- Tile nippers
- Angle grinder
- Margin trowel

- Three-sixteenths-inch V-notched trowel for mosaic flooring
- One-quarter inch V-notched trowel for shower walls
- Clean cloths
- Several five-gallon buckets
- White or gray latex-modified thinset
- Unmodified thinset
- Water
- Grout sponges
- Grout sealer
- Grout sealer applicator

of time researching styles and materials that appeal to you. Visit tile showrooms, look through books and magazines, tour model homes and watch home design specials on TV. Keep a camera and notebook handy, and when a unique space presents itself, snap a few photos and jot some notes. Pull together a notebook including all of your ideas, photos, and clippings, and eventually the perfect look will emerge.

Once you have an idea of what you want to accomplish in your space, get ready to start seriously planning. Take a close look at the area you wish to tile. If you are remodeling, this task will be much easier than if you are in the middle of a new build. Grab your measuring tape, graph paper, and pencil and draw your room to scale. Include renderings of all areas to be tiled—floors,

wainscoting, vanity tops, and shower walls. With tracing paper overlays and colored pencils, sketch several different designs, changing up the size, shape, pattern, and color of your tile. Insert borders and accents to assist in discovering the ideal layout. Once you have a clearer vision of what you want, make a trip to your local tile store and seek out a range of samples. Bring home collections that include field tiles and decorative pieces and place them in their intended location. Place floor tiles on the floor and lean wall tiles against the wall; then take a few steps back. Observing your selection in the room and lighting where it will eventually be placed will help greatly.

Once you have decided on the tile and design, it is time to estimate the amount you will need and place your order. Take careful measurements and add an extra 10 percent for waste, odd cuts, break-age, and future repairs. Before you do the demolition work on your bathroom, be sure that your tile is on-site and has been thoroughly checked for any breakage, that the amount is correct, and that the color is consistent. The last thing you want to do is start a project with only a portion of tile on-site, as any problems will cause delays, often significant ones. In the meantime, while you are waiting for your tile to arrive, go ahead and gather all of the materials you will need for demolition, substrate preparation, setting the tile, and finishing the job.

Step 2: Get ready to tile. To ready your bathroom for tiling, you must remove the existing layer of materials. This means pulling up floors and tearing out old surrounds or tile work. Depending on what you have in place, demolition may be a breeze or a major headache. It is important to remember that some older homes may include haz-ardous materials such as asbestos. If you have any doubt about what type of tile you will be pulling up and tossing out, consult a specialist. Even if you are certain you will not come in contact with toxic materials, be certain to wear safety gear when taking on any demolition project. This includes eye protection, ear protection, a small dust particle mask, work gloves, knee pads, and a back brace.

This particular project simply required the removal of the plumbing fixtures, followed by the plastic surround that had been glued to the underlying plaster walls. Using a pry bar and hammer, we dislodged the surround and then used a razor-blade wall scraper to remove the remaining adhesive residue. Each remodeling situation will be different, and you may be faced with the more difficult task of removing old tile from the shower walls. In this case, cover your tub with a heavy-duty drop cloth to protect it and start breaking away the old tile with a hammer and chisel. Place a large trash bin close by, where you can toss tiles

as they come down. Once you have removed the surround, evaluate the walls for plumb, flatness, and any areas that may need repairs or patching.

Step 3: Prepare the substrate. Once the shower walls are deemed sturdy, flat, and clean, it is time to prepare them to receive tile. There are several ways to create a waterproof substrate for tile, including a thick-set mud bed, a combination of moisture barrier and concrete backer board, or a new innovative product called Kerdi. Because our project was a remodel, and we wanted to keep the thickness of the shower walls to a minimum, we chose to work with the Kerdi system.

When you see the glow of bright orange, you know it must be Kerdi. Kerdi is a thin, light-weight, easy-to-use waterproof membrane with limited crack-suppressing abilities. Used on both floors and walls, Kerdi is composed of soft poly-ethylene, covered on both sides by anchoring fleece webbing. Once Kerdi is in place, tiles are set directly over the membrane using the thinset method.

Installing Kerdi

A. Prepare the substrate to receive Kerdi. Be sure walls are sturdy, load-bearing, flat, and free from moisture and debris. It is important that Kerdi be able to adhere properly to the underlying substrate, which can be any number of materials, including drywall, greenboard, plaster, and plywood.

B. Measure shower walls, noting cutouts for plumbing. With a tape measure, straight edge, and pencil, transfer these measurements to the roll of Kerdi. Using scissors, cut the Kerdi membrane to size, allowing for an additional two inches to overlap at the corners. Instead of overlapping the material, you may also chose to abut panels at each juncture, and seam the open corners with Kerdi band (precut strips).

C. With a one-quarter inch by three-sixteenths-inch V-notched trowel, apply a

bond coat of white or gray thinset made to adhere to the substrate (normally latex-modified thinset). Press the Kerdi into the mortar. Work it into place using the flat side of the trowel, smoothing out all air bubbles with diagonal sweeping motions.

D. Once the Kerdi has adequately bonded and cured, you may then tile directly over the membrane, using a gray or white latex-modified thinset.

Step 4: Set the tile. Begin this step by checking your tub for level (many tubs slope to some degree). At the lowest spot of the tub, mark the height of a full tile. Draw a level line around the tub at that height. This will become your working line. If your tub is not completely level, you will have to make tapered cuts in the first course of tile to create a level line. To speed things along, go ahead and cut the tiles for the first row before spreading the thinset.

Starting with the most visible wall (usually the back wall), set the first row of tile. Use the appropriate size of notched trowel (generally to match the thickness of your tile) and modified thinset. We used a one-quarter inch **V**-notched trowel for our application. Check for level often, and shim the tiles as needed. It is imperative that this first row of tile be exactly level, or the rest of your installation will be skewed. (A common alternate method to begin tiling is to screw a ledger board to the wall at your level line and start tiling with the second course. You would then install the bottom row at the end of the project, custom-cutting each tile as needed.)

Using three-by-six-inch subway tile allowed us to set a full tile at one end of the shower wall, and almost exactly half a tile at the opposite end (you want to avoid any cuts that result in less than half a tile, if possible, for the best look). Each row of tile is staggered, due to the brick pattern. To maintain a symmetrical staggered pattern, measure and mark

the center of a tile, and align that mark with the grout line of the preceding row. Work your way up the wall, checking each row for level and plumb, and occasionally pulling a tile off to check for complete thinset coverage. Use a hole saw with a diamond-coated tip or an angle grinder with a diamond blade to cut the tiles around plumbing fixtures as needed, making the smallest holes possible and keeping in mind that most plumbing fixtures have a sleeve or flange that will hide part of the cut.

After completing the field tiles on the back wall, move to the side walls, completing one before moving to the other. Use the same procedure to set the side walls as for the back wall, allowing about an eighth of an inch where each wall meets as an expansion joint that will later be filled with flexible caulk. Take your time measuring cuts, paying particular attention to the most visible areas. You will need to install a bullnose trim on the two side walls for a finished look. Because the Kerdi underlayment is very thin, we were able to install two-by-six-inch surface bullnose trim pieces on the outer edge, instead of the commonly used radius bullnose.

Once all three walls have received the field tile, set the accent border. Using a utility knife, cut the appropriate size strips from the black-and-white mosaic sheets (we chose a width of three squares). Set the border in place around the top perimeter, capping the subway tiles. Ensure that the checkerboard pattern is maintained along the entire expanse. To complete this portion of the project, install the crown molding, mitering each corner at a 45-degree angle (best accomplished with a wet saw that features an adjustable fence to create a 45-degree angle). You can choose to purchase crown molding end caps for a nice finished look, or opt to miter the outer corners back onto themselves to form the end cap.

Step 5: Grout the tile. The narrow grout joints employed in this tile project require the use

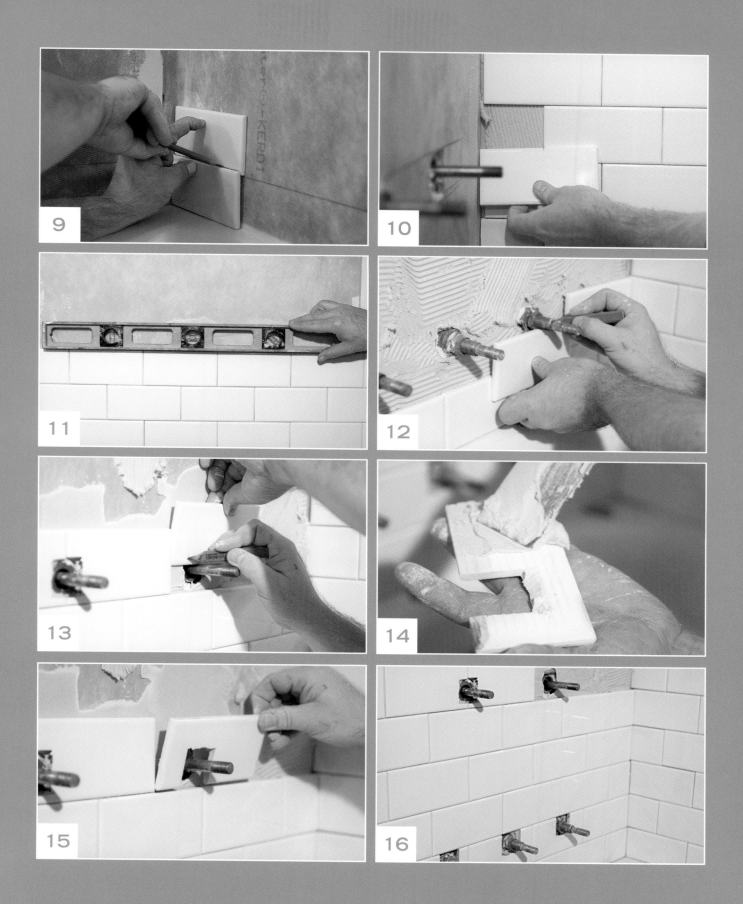

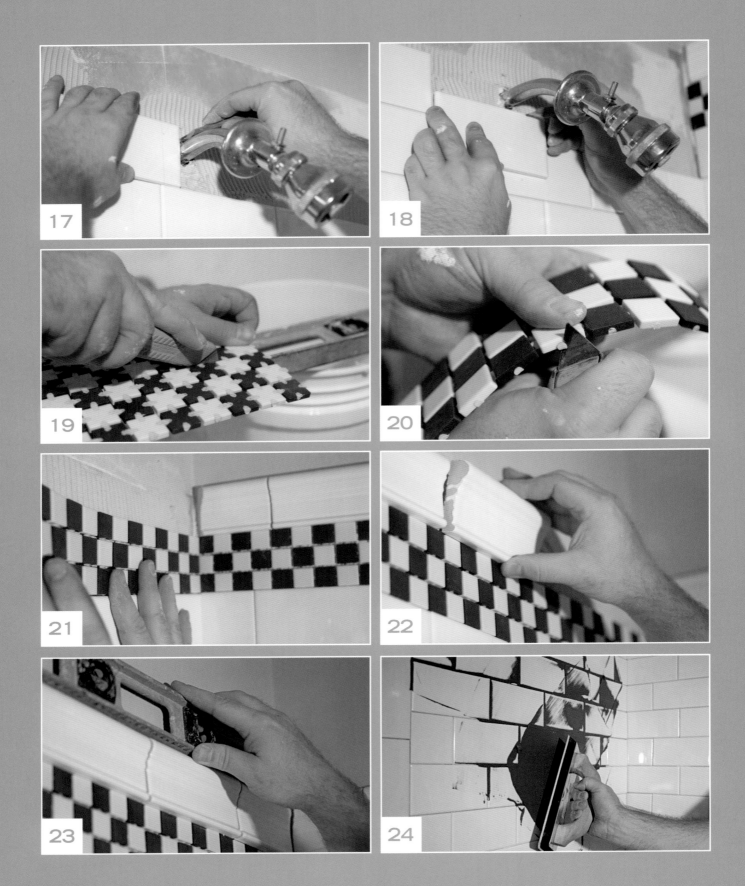

of nonsanded grout. We chose gray for a classic look, and to lessen the likelihood of future discoloration. It is imperative that you apply a penetrating sealer to any unglazed tiles prior to grouting to ease cleanup and prevent staining (our black-and-white border strip and crackle-finish molding required sealing). Once the tiles have cured (at least twenty-four hours), it is time to grout. Mix the powdered grout with water per the manufacture's directions, blending by hand with a margin trowel to a consistency that will not pour (similar to peanut butter). Allow the mixture to slake for about ten minutes. Using a rubber grout float, spread the grout diagonally, back and forth, up and down, forcing it into the joints. Tilt the float 90 degrees to the tile and use the edge to remove excess grout, which will leave the tiles nearly clean. Use a slightly damp sponge to tool the grout into the joints for an even look, then allow the grout to dry for ten to twenty minutes. After the grout has started to set up slightly and a haze begins to form, use a lightly damp sponge to clean, sweeping in diagonal motions across the joints. Be sure to empty and refill buckets with clean water often to prevent reapplication of the haze. Once the tiles are clean and the grout sufficiently dry, buff tiles with a soft dry cloth.

Step 6: Seal the tile. Once the grout has cured (approximately forty-eight hours), seal it well, using a penetrating sealer. There are a variety of applicators on the market to make this an easy task. Be sure to buff any remaining sealer from the field tile as you move along with a dry cloth. Plan to reapply the sealer every few years as part of a routine maintenance regimen.

The Floor

Step 1: Plan your layout. Measure the floor space to be tiled. Transfer these measurements to a piece of graph paper to begin designing your lay-out. Estimate the amount of tile needed and add extra for unusual cuts or future repairs. Our design featured one-inch unglazed porcelain hexagon mosaic, supplied in twelve-by-twenty-four-inch sheets. You may want to consider a contrasting or decorative border for your project. Make your plans for that here in this stage.

Step 2: Get ready to tile and prepare the substrate. Using proper safety equipment, remove all baseboards, plumbing fixtures, toilets, and inward-swinging doors. Remove the existing floor covering and evaluate the substrate for damage and over-all condition. Ensure that the substrate is sturdy, level, and does not flex. For our project, we chose to use Schlüter Systems' Ditra over the existing plywood as our underlayment, in place of cement backer board.

Ditra is a polyethylene membrane featuring a grid structure of square cavities, anchored by a layer of fleece on its underside. It is used as an underlayment to ceramic and natural stone tile for uncoupling, waterproofing, and as a vapor pressure equalization layer. Ditra is an eighth of an inch thick and replaces the need for cement backer board. It can be used over plywood, concrete, mortar screeds, radiant heating, masonry (such as brick and stone), existing tile floors, existing syn-thetic floors in good repair, plywood, and oriented strand board (OSB). Ditra cannot be used over cushioned resilient flooring, luan, or particleboard.

Installing Ditra

A. Measure the area to receive Ditra. Transfer your measurements to the roll. Be sure to plan cutouts around fixtures and plumbing. Using scissors, cut the Ditra to fit your space.

B. Once you have dry-fitted the Ditra, apply bonding mortar suitable for the sub-strate (generally a latex-modified thinset). Mix the thinset to a soupy or fluid consistency. Using a three-sixteenths-inch **V**-notched trowel, apply the

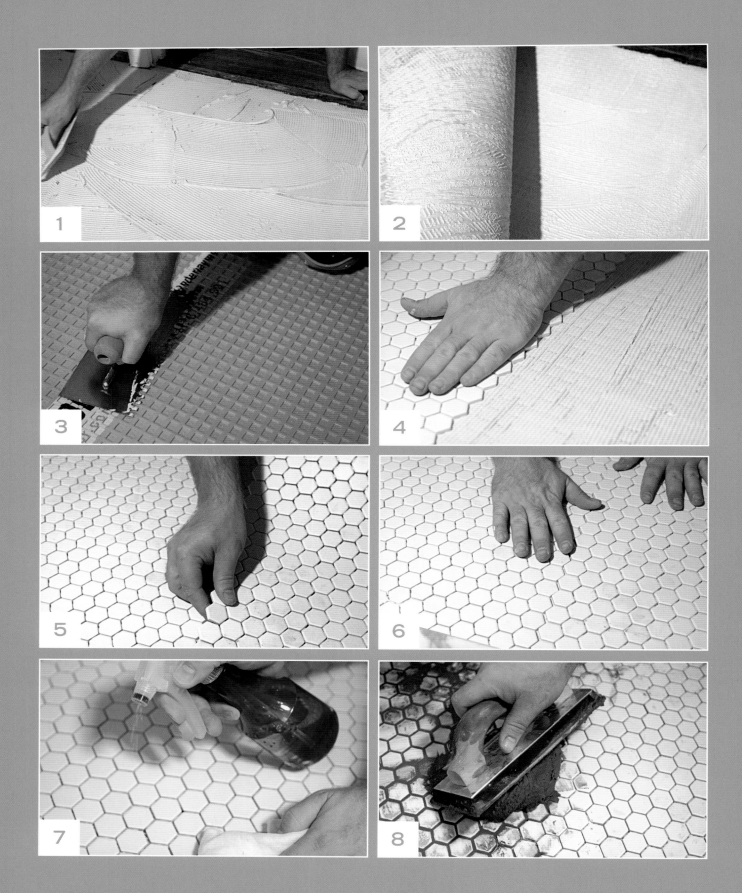

bond coat to your substrate. Do not be concerned with the direction of the trowel marks.

C. Next, press the Ditra into the mortar, using the flat side of a float or trowel. Pull back the corners to check for complete mortar coverage. Where seams are required, simply abut the edges.

D. Once the Ditra is in place, there is no need to wait to begin tiling, you may do so right away. Use unmodified thinset with a trowel notched in a suitable size for the thickness of your tile.

Step 3: Set the tile. Measure to find the center point of your room. Snap intersecting chalk lines. Be sure that your lines are square. If your walls are significantly out of square, use the 3-4-5 method (*see "Determining Square Using the 3-4-5 Method" in chapter 8*) to create square working lines. Plan to place any tapered cuts in the less visible areas of the room. Next, lay out the tile and begin dry-fitting and making cuts, generally starting with the most visible area. Starting at the door and along the tub (the most visible areas of our small bath), we spread unmodified thinset per the Ditra manufacturer's directions, using a three-sixteenths-inch **V**-notched trowel. Be sure to work in small areas, ideally within arm's reach. Gently lay the mosaic onto the thinset, pressing the tile down lightly so as not to force the thinset up through the tile joints. You may also use a covered wooden block and mallet to tap each sheet into place. Carefully lay the adjoining sheets in a similar fashion, aligning the tiles for a continuous pattern. Allow for a eighth-inch expansion joint at the perimeter, where the tiles meet differing materials. You will fill these areas later with flexible caulk. Adjust each mosaic sheet as needed as you move along, avoiding any obvious grid patterns. The flooring should appear as a solid sheet of tile. Allow a minimum of twenty-four hours for the tile to cure before moving on to the next step of grouting.

Step 4: Grout the tile. The small grout joints associated with mosaic tile require the use of an nonsanded grout. Be sure when working with unglazed porcelain to seal its surface well with a penetrating sealer before grouting, or the tile may stain. Using a margin trowel, mix the grout by hand in a small bucket, according to the manufacturer's directions, to a creamy peanut butter consistency, then allow it to slake for ten minutes. When mixing several batches of grout, be certain to blend them exactly the same each time to maintain consistency in color. Scoop some grout from the bucket onto the floor with the grout float or margin trowel. Begin forcing it into the joints with the float, using a back-and-forth motion at a 45-degree angle to the grout joint. Remove any excess grout by placing the float at a 90-degree angle to the floor. Allow the grout to set up slightly over approximately ten to twenty minutes, and then wipe excess with a lightly damp sponge at a 45-degree angle to the joints. Rinse the sponge in clean water often to prevent reapplication of the haze. Ideally wipe, flip the sponge, wipe again, and rinse. Empty water buckets and refill with fresh clean water frequently. Let the grout set up further and remove any remaining haze with a clean, dry cloth. Caulk the expansion joints at the perimeter of the installation with a flexible caulk, rather than grout.

Step 5: Seal the grout. Once the grout has had time to cure (approximately forty-eight hours), seal the tile and the grout once more with penetrating sealer. If you have selected a glazed tile that does not require sealing, use a special applicator to seal the joints only. Buff any remaining sealer from the surface of the tile with a clean dry cloth. Reapply sealer as needed every few years as part of an ongoing maintenance program.

Before

After

chapter 10 | in the bath

Before

After

chapter 11 | **on the floor**

There's just no way around it; floors take significant abuse, often experiencing the greatest wear and tear of any part of the home, exposed to the rigors of high heels, pet's claws, and children's toys. At the same time, the color, pattern, and texture of flooring has a powerful influence on the overall style of a home. Because this quintessential element shoulders such an important responsibility, it makes sense that we strive to select the most durable and aesthetically pleasing material possible.

Certainly, most of us desire flooring that is both pleasing to the eye and hard-wearing. We long for a surface that serves as a foundation to our personal style while allowing for change and adaptation as our tastes fluctuate over the years. Unfortunately, not all flooring material lives up to these exceptional ideals—except perhaps for tile. Tile, whether porcelain, ceramic, or natural stone, when selected with care, can provide a lifetime of beauty underfoot. Stone, with its rich appearance, depth of color, and one-of-a-kind character, is steadfast in its durability. For these reasons, many homeowners place natural stone at the top of their wish list. Unfortunately, most later cross off this luxury item, assuming that it is cost-prohibitive. In actuality, natural stone can be quite affordable, particularly if you install the material yourself. All too often, homeowners might be able to afford the tile itself, but the dream quickly fades when the estimate for labor is presented. Therefore, it is the goal of this chapter to guide you through the installation of stone flooring. If you yearn for the striking beauty of natural stone within your home,

feel confident in your do-it-yourself skills, but feel you cannot afford the material when the installation cost is added, this project is for you.

Take your time, adhere to recommended safety measures, and with a little planning, patience, and perseverance, you can successfully lay a stone tile floor. It is true that laying stone is an art form that does require considerable skill, but give yourself a break if you start thinking your tile setting does not equal that of a seasoned pro. Keep at it, and soon you will be bursting with pride as you step back to admire your hard-earned accomplishment.

In this project, we use honed and filled eighteen-by-eighteen-inch Turkish travertine in classic cream and dark chocolate to update an average-size dining room. The design mimics the look of a large inlaid carpet, thus effectively separating the dining area from the adjoining spaces.

Step 1: Evaluate your space, plan your layout, and gather your materials.

Measure your room and transfer the dimensions to graph paper using a one-quarter inch scale. Play with the design to discover what layout flatters the room best. By using this sketch, you can determine the ideal border size to allow for symmetrical, even cuts within its frame. From there, you can figure the total square footage required for your project, add 10 percent for waste, and order your stone. Take your time on this step, as preparation and planning are key to an artistic and successful tile project.

Once you have planned your layout and made any required adjustments, it is time to order your stone and gather your materials. Be sure to order

laying a stone tile floor

Estimated time to install: Five days, with a partner
Skill level: Advanced, with general tile-setting skills

Materials

- Graph paper
- Ruler
- Tape measure
- Cement board
- Latex-modified thinset (choose the less expensive gray color for setting cement board)
- Cement board fasteners (use the screws recommended by the cement board manufacturer)
- Mesh tape for covering the joints of cement board
- Leveling compound, if needed

- Framing square
- Combination square
- Level
- Margin trowel
- Half-inch square-notched trowel
- Straightedge
- Chalk line
- Pencils
- Utility knife with extra blades
- Wet saw
- Handheld angle grinder with diamond blade
- Belt sander

- Latex-modified medium-bed mortar mix, or marble and granite mix (choose white for setting the stone tile)
- Several five-gallon buckets
- Sponges
- Mixing paddle for half-inch drill
- Nonsanded grout, for grout joints of one-eighth inch or less
- Nonsanded caulk color matched to grout
- Grout float

- Stone shaping tool/rubbing stone (for smoothing any rough edges)
- Masking tape
- Drop cloth
- Safety equipment: knee pads, back support, eye protection, and ear protection
- Wedges or spacers—one-sixteenth inch
- Penetrating sealer made for natural stone
- Spray bottle
- Soft terry cloth towel
- Broom and vacuum

your stone early to ensure it is in stock and delivered before you buy, rent, or borrow the materials noted in the above checklist. If you think there will be more tile projects in your future, consider purchasing some of the high-end tools, such as the angle grinder and wet saw. If this is a one-time project, rent these high-ticket items from a local store. Be sure that all materials are clean and in good repair to ensure smooth progress.

Step 2: Prepare the substrate. The type of subfloor you have will determine the prep work required before you set your tile. If your home rests on a concrete foundation, you will need to check that the concrete has had time to cure (approximately twenty-eight days), and that its surface is true and level. In our project, the sub-

floor is concrete covered with a layer of cement backer board. The backer board was added because of a significant difference in floor height from room to room. Normally, cement backer board is used on top of a wooden subfloor. If you want to install heavy natural stone tile on a wooden substrate, you must be certain that it is sturdy enough to support the added weight and will not flex. Ideally, a wooden subfloor will consist of two layers of three-quarter-inch plywood, topped by half-inch cement backer board. It is important to take into consideration the added height created by the layering of the plywood, cement backer board, and tile (including the thinset used to set the tile), especially in conjunction with adjoining rooms, doorways, and appliances. If you are working

Tips for Ordering and Receiving Natural Stone

Before placing your order, determine how recently your supplier received the samples they are displaying and if they accurately represent the coloration of the current stock available. A tile on display may be several months old, and the quarry may be cutting from a new location, and thus supplying a different shade of stone. To be certain you are getting exactly what you want, it is wise to purchase several full-size samples of the stone you will actually be receiving. If possible, arrange to see an installed application of the stone you are considering. Pictures can be helpful, but nothing beats the real thing.

If you are using a filled (rather than unfilled) travertine, it is important to know that the "fill" produced at the quarry is a combination of travertine dust and epoxy resin. The dust used to manufacture the fill is a by-product of the travertine tiles that have been cut at the quarry. Most of the time, the fill is a good color match; on occasion, however, the fill can appear slightly pink, purple, or even black. If fill match is a major concern, you can always order the stone unfilled and fill the surface depressions with grout in a complementary color. A word of caution: unlike quarry fill, which is extremely strong and results in a perfectly smooth and level surface,

grout used for on-the-job-filled stones may leave slight depressions, and may require additional grout applications.

When you have nailed down the stone for your job, be sure to measure accurately and add a waste factor of at least 10 percent. The actual percentage can vary, depending on the complexity of the installation itself; jobs that require a large number of angles and numerous cuts or insets will result in more waste. A good example is stone laid diagonally, rather than square: because corners must be cut in the diagonal application, there will be some waste, and it will require more stone to cover an identical surface area.

When you receive your stone, inspect it thoroughly to ensure that it has not been damaged during shipment, that tiles appear to be square and reasonably consistent in thickness, and that it is the material you ordered. Your supplier should have already taken the time to explain that stone, being a natural product, can vary dramatically from one tile to the next. Once this explanation has been provided, it is not uncommon for a dealer to request that you sign a disclaimer. These disclaimers generally detail exactly what you should expect as a normal range of variation, and what specifically would justify a return. Because stone is extremely

heavy and can shift during shipment, some minimal breakage should be expected. Generally this will not impact the overall coverage, as these stones can be used in areas that would normally require the stone to be cut anyway. If the breakage is extensive, report it to the dealer, freight carrier, and supplier immediately.

It is common, especially with more porous stones, for the shipment to arrive damp. As a result, the tiles may appear much darker than the samples you selected from. Before you panic and tell your dealer there has been a shipping error, pull several pieces from the crate and allow them to dry. You will probably find that they lighten significantly. On the opposite end of the spectrum, the stone may arrive dusty and dry, and only after cleaning, sealing, and/or color enhancing will it resemble the showroom sample.

If for some reason you are not satisfied with the material once it has been received, or you change your mind altogether regarding your selection, you will more than likely face a 20 to 30 percent restocking fee to cover the cost of returning the shipment to the supplier. Returning stone shipments is a cumbersome and costly job, so make sure that you have done your homework prior to placing your order.

with a plywood foundation, once it is securely screwed in place, install the cement backer board with a gray latex-modified thinset mortar and the fasteners the manufacturer recommends, staggering the joints of each board as you move along. Once the cement board is set, cover the joints with mesh tape and thinset mortar. Be certain to sweep and/or vacuum the cement board prior to setting your tile to ensure adequate adhesion.

Step 3: Get ready to tile. Once you have prepared your subfloor, gathered your setting materials, and the stone is on-site, it's time to get ready to tile! First, sort through your stone tile, making stacks of light, medium, and dark tiles. This will ensure a nice blend throughout the installation. Also, look for any tiles that seem out of square or much too thick, as this will save you headaches as the project progresses.

Now, refer back to your graph paper and prepare to snap chalk reference lines. Using your tape measure, pinpoint the center of the room and mark it. Snap intersecting perpendicular chalk lines using this center point. (Don't be afraid to brush away any chalk lines that are inaccurate and start again.) Measure and mark your outside border. Check that your lines stay square as you go along (*"Determining Square Using the 3-4-5" in chapter 8*).

Step 4: Set the border tile. Working from the square reference lines you have established, you will begin to set the outside border (eighteen-by-eighteen-inch full tile, and six-by-eighteen-inch contrasting stripe). Dry-fit your tiles around a portion of the focal point perimeter to make sure the layout is pleasing to the eye and that cuts at each end are symmetrical. Stone tiles with a flat, square edge should be set with a very tight grout joint, or butt-jointed. You will want to maintain a joint of a sixteenth of an inch or less. If you wish, use one-sixteenth-inch wedge spacers to ensure equal joint spacing. Miter the ends of the

contrasting narrow border where they will meet at each corner. Remember, if your room is out of square, some of the border tiles will need to be tapered at the wall.

Mix the white latex-modified thinset (medium-bed mortar mix or marble and granite mix) with a half-inch electric drill and mortar mixing paddle in a five-gallon bucket. Mix the thinset to a consistency similar to cake frosting; it should just allow the ridges left by the notched trowel to remain standing. You do not want the mortar to be too wet or too dry. Work within a four-foot area (or within arm's reach), spreading the mud with a half-inch notched trowel (or with notches suited to the thickness of the tile you are working with).

For best adhesion, cover the back of each tile with a thin layer of mortar using your trowel (this is called back-buttering). Set the tile in place, pulling it up to check for even mortar coverage (most likely you will be pulling up quite a few tiles to readjust for level). If trowel notches remain visible, add mud to these areas, reset the tile, and press to ensure good contact. Check to see if the tile is level. Add thinset to low areas, and remove thinset in areas that are too high. Set the next tile, repeating the same sequence each time (back-butter, level, adjust as needed).

Be sure to clean the tiles as you move along with a damp sponge, especially the front edges and grout joints. Continue to level each tile as you go, adjusting up or down as needed by adding or removing thinset. Periodically, run your finger down the tile joints to feel for high or low spots. Place your level across several tiles to ensure that there are no lipped grout joints, and that the installation is maintaining level. Continue this procedure as you move along the border.

Step 5: Set the diagonal tile. After the outside border has been set and allowed to dry (twelve hours), prepare to set the interior diagonal portion of your design. For diagonal installations, snap a set of reference lines that intersect at the center of the room to form a 90-degree angle. From the intersecting point of these two lines, measure out equal distance in three directions, and connect these points, extending these lines to form a large X pattern on the floor. These lines are your new reference lines, and are at a 45-degree angles to the original right-angle reference lines you had established (see page 122). You may at this time measure and mark the entire grid to be certain your installation stays right on track. Check your layout to make sure that cuts are symmetrical at all outer edges of the design. To avoid irregular or small diagonal cuts at the border, it is prudent to dry-fit your tile, making adjustments where needed. When dry-fitting your layout, go ahead and cut some of the tiles and set them in place. This allows you to move along much faster once you get started.

To begin setting the tiles, start in the corner of the room that will function as your primary focal point, working your way across the room. Set the tiles as described in the previous section, following the sequence of back-buttering, checking for level, and adding or removing thinset as you go along. Check often for level with the adjoining field tiles as you work.

Step 6: Get ready to grout. Grouting natural stone is much less labor-intensive if you apply a coat of penetrating sealer (grout release) before you start. Grouting a porous material that has not been presealed can be a nightmare, as the stone can wick up the grout, making cleanup difficult at best.

To use a penetrating sealer as a grout release, first clean the floor very well, by sweeping and then going over it once again with a vacuum or shop vac. Place drop cloths or dust mats at each entrance to the room to minimize the reaccumula-tion of dust and dirt. Once the floor is clean, begin sealing by spraying a quality penetrating sealer evenly over the tile, working in small sections at a time. (Sealers for natural stone are available through local home centers, such as Lowe's and Home Depot, or on-line from top manufacturers. Be sure to select a penetrating sealer, not a topcoat, so you do not alter the look of the stone.) Continue to spray on the sealer, wiping off the excess with a clean, soft terry-cloth towel. Repeating these steps until the entire floor has been sealed. Allow to dry completely before grouting (approximately two hours).

Step 7: Grout the tile. After you have sealed the floor and allowed it to dry, you can get ready to grout. Stone tile set with a tight grout joint requires nonsanded grout. For a seamless look, select a complementary color.

To mix the grout, follow the manufacturer's directions, as each product varies. In addition, some manufacturers offer special additives and mixtures that help to prevent mold and mildew growth, and/or ensure the grout color remains steadfast and nonfading. Be sure to look into these options at the time of purchase.

For butt-jointed stone tiles, you do not need to mix a large amount of grout at a time. Ideally, plan to fill one-fifth of a five-gallon bucket with the mixture. Mix the grout by hand with a margin trowel to the consistency of creamy peanut butter or cake frosting. Allow a few minutes for the grout to set up. Then, using your margin trowel, place a scoop or two of grout at your starting point. Use your grout float to press the grout into the joints, then wipe away the excess, holding the float at a 45-degree angle. Work in small sections at a time.

As you go along, take a damp (not wringing wet) sponge and wipe the tile surface to ease grout haze removal. Wipe the tile at a 45-degree angle, flip the sponge, wipe again, and then rinse the

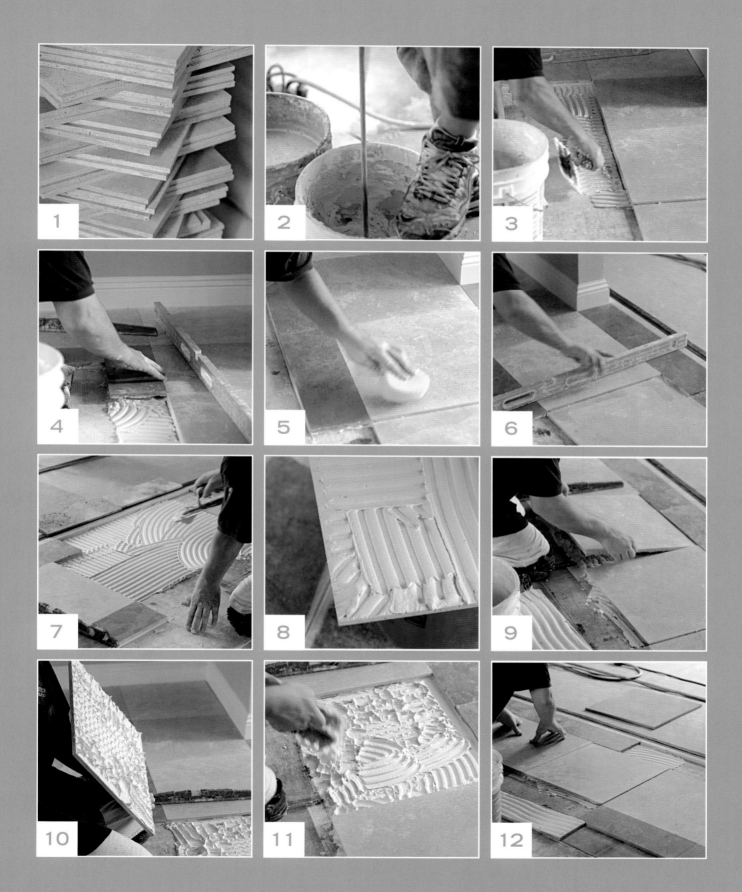

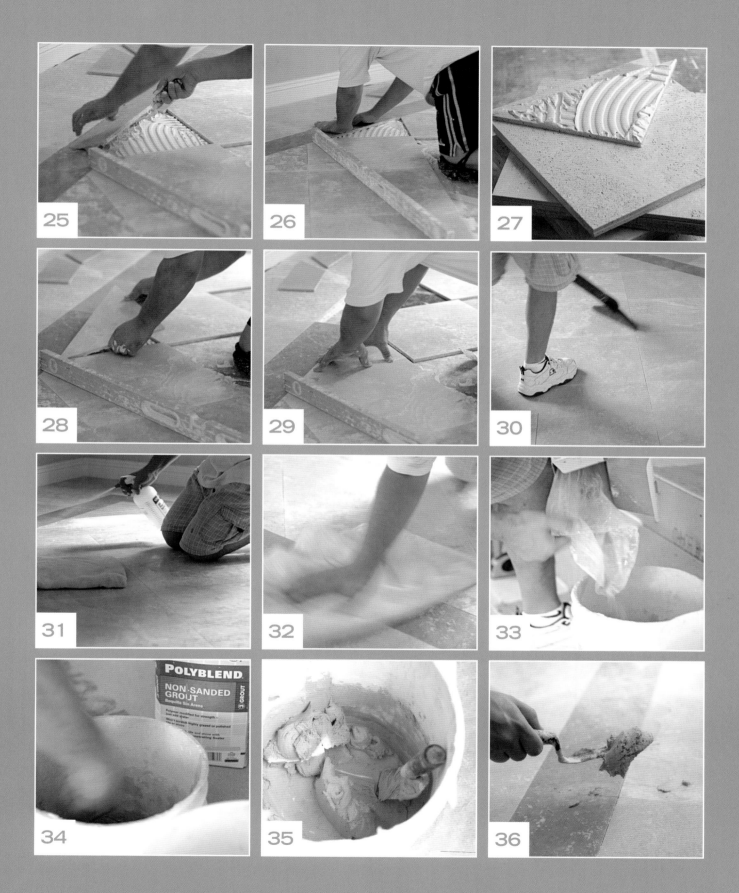

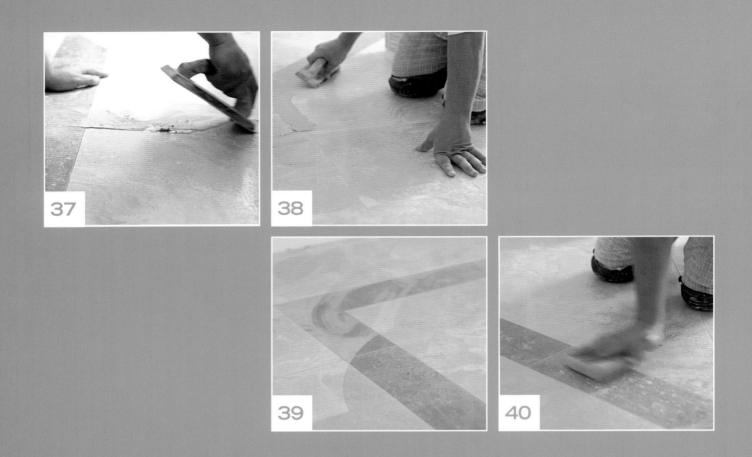

sponge thoroughly (wipe, flip, wipe, rinse). Switch to a clean bucket of water routinely as to not waste time adding haze back to the floor. Continue this process of grouting and cleaning until you have grouted the entire floor. Allow the grout time to dry (approximately forty-eight hours) before moving on to the next step.

Step 8: Seal the tile and finish up.

Once you have grouted the entire floor and it is 100 percent haze free, clean it well once more by sweeping and vacuuming. Now you will apply the final coats of sealer. You are almost there! (How are your knees and back holding up?) Remember,

any dirt or grout haze will forever remain embedded in the final coats of sealer, so be very particular about the cleanliness of the tile.

As you did in Step 5, spray on a quality penetrating sealer, working in small sections, wiping away any excess. Apply two coats in this manner to seal both the tile and the grout sufficiently. After the coats have dried, your tile project is just about done. At this point, fill the joints at the walls with a caulk color matched to your grout, replace baseboards and shoe molding, and you are done! Congratulations!

Glossary

accelerators: Additives used to speed the setup of mortar.

acid-washed stone: Stone treated with acidic substances to accelerate the aging process.

aerography: A decorative technique in which ceramic color is sprayed or blown onto the tile surface.

ashlar pattern: A random setting pattern using various sizes of square and rectangular tile, which gives an Old World effect.

ASTM: Acronym for The American National Standards Institute which establishes guidelines and performance levels for ceramic tile in the United States.

back-butter: The process of slathering the back of a stone tile with thinset material to ensure proper mortar coverage. This prevents hollow areas and subsequent future cracking of tiles. Also helpful to ensure a level installation.

backerboard: Ready made substrate for setting tile. Also known as cement board or CBU (cementous backer unit).

backsplash: The area located between the countertop and lower cabinet, normally sixteen to eighteen inches in height.

batten: A strip of wood used to support vertical tiles as they cure.

bicottura: Italian for "twice fired." A tile is fired to form bisque, then fired again to fuse the glaze.

biscuit: A fire-hardened slab of clay.

bisque: A fired, unglazed clay body.

bluestone: A hard metamorphic sandstone quarried in the United States, commonly found in shades of blue, violet, and buff.

border: A decorative piece of tile, often long and narrow, set within field tiles to create interest.

brick pattern: A method of setting rectangular tiles in a staggered or offset fashion, thus creating the look of a brick wall.

brushed finish: A finish obtained by brushing the stone's surface with a coarse wire rotary brush, often giving it a leathery appearance.

bullnose: A trim tile with a rounded edge.

bush-hammered finish: A finish created by mechanically beating a stone's surface to give it a subtle or dramatic texture.

butt-joint: When tiles are set tightly together with minimal grout joints it is referred to as butt-jointing.

calibrated tile: A stone tile that has been machine-cut on both sides, offering a precise thickness.

caulk: A compound used to seal tile seams and joints to prevent water infiltration as well as offer a flexible material at expansion joints.

cement backer board: A dimensionally stable Portland cement–based panel used to create a water-resistant substrate.

cement body tile: A tile made from Portland cement and sand.

cement mortar: A mixture of Portland cement, sand, other ingredients, and water, used to bond tiles to a substrate.

chamfer: A beveled tile edge.

checkerboard pattern: Alternating square tiles of differing colors or shades.

chiseled edge: A mechanically chipped tile edge, resulting in a rustic, aged appearance.

cladding: Facing a wall in a stone.

clay: A substance made up of a variety of ingredients, such as kaolin, quartz, sand, aluminum silicates, and traces of minerals such as mica, feldspar, and iron.

cleavage: The natural splitting point of a stone mass.

cleft finish: A finish created by the quarry method of splitting the material along its natural plane, leaving its surface rough. Normally associated with slate.

cobblestone: A stone that appears naturally rounded or distressed, due to many years of use or weathering.

coefficient of friction: A guideline established by the ASTM which determines how much effort is required to move an object across the surface of a tile, wet or dry. Helpful in choosing tiles based upon their slip resistance.

coquina: A limestone comprised of seashells and calcite, primarily extracted in Florida.

cove tile: A tile trim that smoothly rounds out a 90-degree inside or outside corner, or creates a transition between horizontal and vertical tiled surfaces.

crazing: Fine cracks across the face of a tile, often created deliberately to give it an aged look.

cross-cutting: The process of cutting a block of stone parallel to the natural bedding plane, giving the new surface a mottled or cloudlike appearance.

cure time: The time required for thinset used to set tile to become hard.

delftware: Blue-and-white-painted Dutch earthenware.

dust pressed: Tiles are formed from nearly dry clay ingredients under extreme pressure.

eased edge: A softened edge on a tile, as opposed to a sharp square edge, used for safety.

efflorescence: A white powderlike substance on the surface of tile or grout, often a result of the accumulation of salts due to excessive moisture.

encaustic tiles: Hard-wearing, artistic tiles with designs carved or stamped on them, then filled with liquid clay called slip. This technique originated in thirteenth-century medieval Europe.

epoxy grout: A two-part grout system consisting of epoxy resin and epoxy hardener, which offers stain resistance, chemical resistance, and colorfast qualities.

etched finish: A decorative surface finish created by a variety of methods, most often with abrasive chemicals or sandblasting.

expansion joint: A joint filled with flexible material that allows for movement where tile meets another surface, and thus prevents cracking and buckling.

extruded tile: Tile created by forcing a clay mixture through a die, resulting in a continuous ribbon of clay that is then cut into individual tiles with a wire cutter or similar tool.

faience: A colorful tin-glazed ceramic with a flawless glasslike appearance, named for its town of origin, Faenza, Italy.

field stone: A stone found above ground, normally worn and weathered.

filled stone: Stone with its open pores prefilled with a stone-dust resin or epoxy at the factory. Travertine is one stone that is commonly filled.

flagstone: Thick, flat stone in various shapes, used to pave walkways, driveways, or patios.

flamed finish: A very rough-textured surface achieved through direct exposure to intense heat and flame. Normally associated with granite.

flashing: Markings that appear on tile as a result of chemical reactions between inbedded oxides in the clay and the heat of the kiln.

fleuri cut: The process of cutting the stone parallel to the bedding plane. The effect is a cloudlike or mottled appearance.

forty-five: Another way of describing diagonal setting patterns (since lines are set at a 45-degree angle).

fossil: Ancient plant or animal remains preserved within a material such as stone.

gang saw: A large wet saw that cuts raw blocks of stone down into a specified thickness.

gauged: Ground by machine to a uniform thickness.

glaze: Liquid glass created from silica plus pigments or colorants, chemically bonded to the tile body through extremely high temperatures.

granite: A hard, crystalline, igneous rock formation formed when various minerals such as feldspar and quartz are fused by extreme heat.

greenware: Leather-hard clay that has not been through the kiln-firing process.

grout: A cement or epoxy-based material used to fill joints between tiles. Available in a large range of colors.

guillotine cut: A method of cutting a stone tile, most often slate, that creates a ragged and chipped edge.

herringbone pattern: Rectangular tiles set on a slant, forming a zigzag effect.

honed finish: A satin-smooth finish with a flat or matte appearance, as opposed to the glassy finish of polished stone.

igneous rock: Rock formed from molten matter that has cooled and solidified.

impervious tile: Tile that absorbs 0.5 percent or less of its weight in water joint.

inserts: Decorative tiles or accents set into the area where four field tiles meet, or creatively placed in the center of a stone tile.

intaglio: Reverse relief.

kaolin: Clay that fires to a white color.

kiln: The oven used to fire clay.

latex: A water emulsion of either synthetic rubber or plastic, created through polymerization, and used to enhance the bond strength and flexibility of mortar.

lath: Wood strip or metal mesh used to reinforce a mud bed.

lead glaze: A glossy transparent glaze made from lead.

limestone: A rock formed from the sedimentary process, underground and underwater, comprised primarily of calcium deposits of shell and bone.

liner: A long, narrow piece of decorative tile placed within a field of stone to add interest or break up a pattern.

lippage: A difference in height between two adjoining tiles. Industry standards allow for one-sixteenth of an inch in height variance between tiles.

listello: A tile used as a border.

majolica: Brightly colored earthenware covered with a white tin glaze, and featuring decorative painting.

mastic: Premixed thinset tile adhesive with a latex or petrochemical base.

metamorphic rock: Rock altered in appearance by intense pressure, heat, or a combination of both.

monocottura: Italian for "single-fired"; the clay and glaze of monocottura tiles have been fired simultaneously.

mortar: The material used to set stone tile, composed of water, cement, sand, and lime.

mosaic: A field of tiles created from numerous small, often irregular pieces, which may be set to create a pattern or picture.

ninety: A tile placed perpendicular to the wall or in a square fashion (at 90 degrees) may be referred to as on the ninety.

nominal size: A tile size used for general reference, which does not correspond exactly to the tile's actual measurements.

nonvitreous tile: Low-fired tile that can absorb up to and greater than 7 percent of its weight in water.

notched trowel: A handheld tool with square or **V**-shaped notches in various sizes, used to apply mortar.

onyx: A banded, translucent form of marble, found in caves.

pallet: The strong wooden frame on which stone tiles are normally shipped from overseas.

parquetry: An inlaid floor in which two or more tile types or colors create geometric shapes.

patina: Surface changes in the color or texture of a material due to age or exposure to various elements.

paver: A tile shaped by molding; can be low-fired terra-cotta or impervious porcelain.

pillowed: Featuring softly rounded edges.

plumb: True perpendicular.

plywood: Wood sheets laminated together with glue, often used as a substrate for tile installations.

polished finish: A shiny high-gloss finish, normally found on hard stones. This finish draws out the deepest color and full character of a stone.

porcelain: High-fired white clay that has been manufactured by the dust-pressed method.

primary clay: A clay found where it was actually formed.

quarry: A physical location where raw blocks of stone, or other stone deposits, are removed from the earth.

quarry tile: Extruded vitreous or semivitreous floor tiles, usually with an unglazed red body.

quartzite: A stone composed primarily of the mineral quartz and sandstone.

relief: A three-dimensional design on the surface of a tile.

rubber trowel: A tool made from synthetic rubber, used to spread and force grout into joints and remove excess grout.

rug pattern: An inlaid floor design in which various materials make a pattern that resembles a throw rug placed on the floor.

sandblasted finish: A rough surface texture achieved through a high-pressure blast of sand.

sandstone: Rock formed by the sedimentary process, consisting primarily of quartz cemented together by calcium carbonate or silica.

saw cut: A rough surface finish, often exposing saw marks from the stone's initial cutting. Highly slip resistant, it is more rustic in appearance than honed or polished stone.

sealer: Liquid coating applied to the surface of a tile or grout to protect it.

secondary clay: A clay that has been removed from its primary place of formation.

second-grade tile: Ceramic tile with cosmetic defects, which do not affect the wear of the tile.

semivitreous tile: High-fired clay tile, with a water absorption rate between 3 and 7 percent.

serpentine: A stone composed primarily of hydrous magnesium silicate, usually with a dull green color and mottled appearance.

slab: A linear piece of stone cut from the original quarried block.

slate: A rock composed of shale and clay.

slip: Liquid clay.

soapstone: A soft stone composed primarily of talc, chlorite, and often magnetite.

split face: A finish that exhibits a rough, chiseled face, similar to a raw block of stone fresh from the quarry.

stoneware: Fine-textured vitreous or semivitreous ceramic ware.

terra-cotta: Molded nonvitreous tile, commonly red, brown, buff, rust, or pink in color.

terrazzo: A mixture of Portland cement, sand, and marble chips.

thinset: A tile installation method that bonds tiles to a substrate with a thin bed of mortar rather than the thick bed once more common.

tile mural: A painting or picture created with tiles. Used for a focal point or decoration.

tin glaze: A transparent lead glaze to which tin has been added to form an opaque white glaze.

transfer painting: A process in which prints are taken from wood blocks, or copper plates, and then transferred to thin paper using oiled ceramic color as ink. The paper is placed ink side down, then rubbed and soaked off, leaving the design.

travertine: Rock created from limestone near hot bubbling springs, which give it its characteristic pitted surface.

tumbled stone: Stone given an aged finish in a tumbling machine or drum, occasionally with the addition of acids or other materials to soften the stone's edges and give its surface a worn look.

underglaze: Painted decoration applied before a transparent glaze is put over it.

undulated: A wavy surface finish, giving stone the appearance of having undergone thousands of years of foot traffic.

unfilled stone: A stone (most commonly travertine) with surface pits and holes that have not been filled with stone-dust resin or epoxy at the factory.

ungauged: Stone cut without strict adherence to uniform thickness.

vapor barrier: A waterproof membrane placed under on-grade concrete slabs.

vein-cut stone: Stone cut perpendicular to the natural bedding plane, enhancing its horizontal vein structure.

vitreous tile: Extremely high-fired tile that absorbs 0.5 to 3 percent of its weight in water.

waterproof membrane: Material, like plastic or tar paper, used to create a waterproof barrier in wet installations, such as a shower.

weathering: Aging of a surface through the effects of weather.

Resources

Ann Sacks
8120 NE 33rd Drive
Portland, OR 97211
PH (800) 278-8453
www.annsacks.com

Dal-tile
7834 CF Hawn Fwy
Dallas, TX 75217
PH (214) 398-1411
www.daltile.com
(Suppliers of: White subway brick
tile, white porcelain hexagon
mosaic, black and white checkerboard mosaic, "In the bath")

Digitile Ltd.
15 Redchurch Street
London E2 7DJ (England)
PH +44 (0)20 7613 2783
www.digitile.co.uk

Edelman Leather
Teddy & Arthur Edelman Limited
80 Pickett District Road
New Milford, CT 06776
PH (800) 886 - TEDY
www.edelmanleather.com

Globus Cork Inc.
PH (718) 742-7264
www.corkfloor.com

Gooseneck Designs
2020 Hughes Shop Rd
Westminster, MD 21158
PH (410) 848-5663
www.gooseneckdesigns.com

**International Wholesale
Tile**
3500 SW 42nd Ave
Palm City, FL 34990
PH (772) 223-0837
www.internationalwholesaletile.com
(Suppliers of: Granite Solutions
Tile "In the kitchen")

Kohler
www.kohler.com

Lowitz and Company
Foundry Art Fine Bronze, Talisman
Tiles and Bronzework Studio
4401 N. Ravenswood Ave.
Chicago, IL 60640
PH (773) 784-2628
www.lowitzandcompany.com
(Suppliers of: White bronze tile
and liner, "In the kitchen")

Marmoleum
Forbo Flooring
PO Box 667 Humboldt Ind. Park
Hazelton, PA 18201
PH (570) 459-0771
www.themarmoleumstore.com

Natural Stone Design
35B Gulf Breeze Pkwy
Gulf Breeze, FL 32561
PH (850) 916-9767
www.naturalstonedesign.com
(Suppliers of: Fern colored glass
mosaic, "In the kitchen")

Oceanside Glass Tile
2293 Cosmos Court
Carlsbad, CA 92009
PH (760) 929- 4082
www.glasstile.com

Paris Ceramics
146 The Merchandise Mart
Chicago, IL 60654
PH (312) 467-9830
www.parisceramics.com

Patrick Tile
701 S. E St
Pensacola, FL 32501
(850) 384-1869
nickpatrick@mchsi.com
(Nick and Jason Patrick Tile
Masons for "On the floor")

**Plasplugs Portable Wet
Saw**
1100 Towbin Ave.
Lakewood, NJ 08701
www.plasplugs.com
(Suppliers of portable wet saw)

Pratt & Larson
1201 SE 3rd Ave.
Portland, OR 97214
PH (503) 231-9464
www.prattandlarson.com

Reese Foret
Artist
www.reeseforet.com

Rupert Scott Ltd

The Glass Studio

Mytton Mill

Montford Bridge

Shrewsbury SY4 1HA (England)

PH 01743 851393

www.rupertscott.com

Schluter Systems

194 Pleasant Ridge Rd.

Plattsburgh, NY 12901

PH (800) 472-4588

www.schluter.com

(Supplier of: KERDI and DITRA

underlayment, "In the bath")

Sonoma Cast Stone

PO Box 1721

Sonoma, CA 95476

PH (888) 807-4234

www.sonomacaststone.com

Sonoma Tile Makers

7750 Bell Rd.

Windsor, CA 95492

www.sonomatilemakers.com

Surving Studios

17 Millsburg Rd

Middletown, NY 10940

Ph (845) 355-1430

www.surving.com

Terra Viva

Strada di Maratta km. 8,700

05036 Narni Scalo (TR) (Italy)

PH (39) 0744 733121

www.terravivasrl.com

Trout Studios

227 Turkey Drive

Dripping Springs, TX 78620

PH (512) 894-0774

www.troutstudios.com

Walker Zanger

8901 Bradley Ave.

Sun Valley, CA 91352

PH (818) 504-0235

www.walkerzanger.com

Wicanders Cork

Amorim Revestimentos

PH 351 227 475 200

www.wicanders.com

**Please visit us at
www.naturalstonedesign.com
for more links to beautiful
tile and stone materials**

Photo Credits

Page 1: Walker Zanger

Page 2: Tim Street-Porter

Pages 6–7 (clockwise from top left):
Surving Studios tile/Heather Adams;
SimonKenny/belle/arcaid.co.uk;
Walker Zanger; Tria Giovan;
TrevorMein/belle/arcaid.co.uk

Page 8: Tria Giovan

Page 9: Robin Stubbert

Page 10: Tim Street-Porter

Page 11: Robin Stubbert

Page 12: Heather Adams

Page 13 (from left): Nonstock/Roger
Mesquita; Nonstock/Philip
Krejcarek; Heather Adams

Page 14: Beateworks.com/
MichelArnaud

Page 15: Tria Giovan

Page 16: Mainstream/Ray Main

Page 17: SimonKenny/belle/
arcaid.co.uk

Page 18: Ann Sacks

Page 20: Beateworks.com/
ScottVanDyke

Page 21 (from top): Tria Giovan; Tria
Giovan; Walker Zanger

Page 22: Tria Giovan

Page 23: Tria Giovan

Page 24–25:
Davidduncanlivingston.com

Page 25: Eric Roth

Page 27: Davidduncanlivingston.com

Page 28: Robin Stubbert

Page 29: Walker Zanger

Page 30: Robin Stubbert

Page 31 (all): Terra Viva

Page 32: Ann Sacks

Page 33: Davidduncanlivingston.com

Page 34: Eric Roth

Page 35: Eric Roth

Page 37: Beateworks.com/
Tim Street-Porter

Page 38: Beateworks.com/
Brad Simmons

Page 40: Talisman Tiles,
Lowitz and Company/Ann Sacks

Page 41: Tria Giovan

Page 42: Ann Sacks

Page 43: AlanWeintraub/arcaid.co.uk
Architecture by Richard Crisman
and Jeff Brock

Page 45: AlanWeintraub/arcaid.co.uk

Page 46: Beateworks.com/
Tim Street-Porter

Page 48–49: Robin Stubbert

Page 49: Wicanders Cork

Page 50: RichardPowers/arcaid.co.uk

Page 51: Mainstream: Ray Main

Page 52 (all): Globus Cork

Page 53: (left) Beateworks.com/
PieterEstersohn; (right) Ann Sacks

Page 54: Mainstream/Ray Main

Page 56: Mainstream/Ray Main

Page 57: Mainstream/Ray Main

Page 58: Nonstock: Echos

Page 59 (all): Heather Adams

Page 60–61: Tim Street-Porter

Page 61: Tim Street-Porter

Page 64: (left) Oceanside Glass Tile;
(right) Foundry Art, Lowitz and
Company/Ann Sacks

Page 65: (right) Kim Sargent; (left,
from top) Foundry Art, Lowitz and
Company, Sonoma Cast Stone,
Oceanside Glass Tile/Ann Sacks

Page 66: Foundry Art, Lowitz and
Company/Ann Sacks

Page 67: Beateworks.com/
Tim Street-Porter

Page 68: Davidduncanlivingston.com

Page 69: Davidduncanlivingston.com

Page 70: Tria Giovan

Page 71: Eric Roth

Page 72: Tria Giovan

Page 75: Robin Stubbert

Page 76 (all): Heather Adams

Page 78: Laurie Black

Page 79: Tria Giovan

Page 80: Walker Zanger

Page 81 (from top): Sonoma Tile
Makers; Walker Zanger;
Pratt & Larson

Page 82 (from top): Ann Sacks;
Walker Zanger; Ann Sacks

Page 82–83: Walker Zanger

Page 84: (left) Beateworks.com/Richard
Leo Johnson; (right)
Beateworks.com/Brad Simmons

Page 87: Walker Zanger

Page 88: Tria Giovan

Page 89: Ann Sacks

Page 90: Tria Giovan

Page 91: Walker Zanger

Page 92: Walker Zanger

Page 93: Tim Street-Porter

Page 94: Walker Zanger

Page 95: Walker Zanger

Page 100–165 (all): Heather Adams

Page 192: Robin Stubbert

MATERIAL	PROS	CONS
Ceramic	Available in a huge variety of sizes, colors, shapes, and textures for use in the kitchen and bath and on the floor. Numerous matching trims and borders available for a professional-looking job. Ceramic floor tiles do not rot, fade, stain, scratch, or burn. Ceramic tile is extremely durable, easy to install and maintain, and affordable.	Cold and hard underfoot, though the addition of radiant heating and soft area rugs alleviates this problem. Certain surface finishes can be slippery when wet. Grout should be sealed to prevent staining. Requires a strong subfloor.
Porcelain	Endless options in size, color, shape, texture, and pattern. Ideal for floors, walls, and countertops. Manufactured in large formats with rectified edges that allow tile to be set tightly like natural stone. Styles available closely resemble stone, wood, metal, terracotta, and numerous other materials. High-fired for extreme durability. Easy to care for.	Hard and cold underfoot, which can be remedied through radiant heating and soft area rugs. Because of its hardness, porcelain is best cut with a wet saw. Can be more difficult to install than ceramic when using a tight grout joint. Unglazed porcelain must be sealed to prevent staining. Subfloor must be strong. More expensive than basic ceramic.
Limestone	Limestone makes an ideal countertop surface in its harder, denser varieties, which resemble granite in their durability. Ideal for floors and in the bathroom, as it offers sure footing when wet. Good for showers. Easy to care for. Becomes more attractive with use over the years.	Soft, porous, limestone can scratch, etch, and stain much more easily than the dense varieties. Sealing helps to prevent staining, but will not solve problems with scratching and etching. Penetrating sealer should be applied to countertops, floors, and wet areas. Not recommended for outdoor flooring in areas prone to freezing. Takes skill to install attractively. Requires a strong and rigid subfloor. Costs somewhat more than travertine.
Marble	Offers classic, elegant beauty. Its smooth, polished surface is ideal for baking and rolling out dough. Over time an attractive soft matte patina will emerge if marble is left to age naturally. Perfect for special rooms such as the study, home office, and powder bath.	Polished marble can scratch, etch, and stain. On interior floors, dirt and sand will dull its finish over time. Not recommended for outdoor flooring due to a high slip factor when wet. In showers, polished marble will etch with acidic shampoos, and water spots will be magnified. To avoid many of the problems of polished marble, consider a honed or aged finish. Requires a strong and rigid subfloor. Pricey.

MATERIAL	PROS	CONS
Travertine	Travertine is appropriate for countertops if you stick to the hard and dense varieties. It can be ordered factory filled for a smooth and even surface. Ideal for floors, in the bathroom, and in wet areas. Good for showers. Becomes more attractive over the years with use. Reasonable in cost.	Soft, porous travertine can scratch, etch and stain much more easily than the hard, dense varieties. Sealing the stone helps to prevent staining, but will not solve problems with scratching and etching. Penetrating sealer should be applied to countertops, high-traffic floors, and in wet areas. Not recommended for outdoor flooring in areas prone to freezing temperatures. Very large tiles are cumbersome to install. Requires a strong and rigid subfloor.
Granite	Ideal for countertops in the kitchen and bath. Resists scratching, scorching, and etching from acids. Can be used for indoor and outdoor flooring, even in climates that experience freezing.	Granite can stain. Highly porous granites must be sealed. When used as flooring, polished finishes can be extremely slippery when wet. Select a honed, flamed, or brushed finish for wet areas. Requires a strong subfloor. Pricey
Slate	As a countertop material, slate does not react with acidic substances, and it resists staining. It can take significant abuse as a flooring material, and its inherent color variations camouflage dirt. Ideal in bathrooms and on exterior porches, as it offers sure footing when wet. One of the most affordable natural stones.	Natural cleft slate can become a nuisance when used as a countertop, due to its uneven surface. To ensure a lifetime of beauty, seal with a penetrating sealer. Ungauged material can be difficult to install. Requires a strong and rigid subfloor.
Brick	Ideal for floors and walls. Extremely durable and will withstand significant abuse. Easy to install and care for.	Hard underfoot. Must be sealed to prevent staining. Requires a strong subfloor.
Terra-cotta	Available in a wide range of color tones, sizes, and shapes. Ages wonderfully. Some types are very cost friendly.	Must be sealed to prevent staining. Not recommended for outdoor flooring in areas prone to freezing. Some types are more difficult to install due to irregularities in size, shape, and thickness. Requires a strong and rigid subfloor.

MATERIAL	PROS	CONS
Cork	Soft, quiet, and warm underfoot. Excellent insulator and sound barrier. Antistatic and antiallergenic. Good for bathrooms and basements. Environmentally friendly. Ages well. Some types take on the appearance of more expensive materials such as travertine, wood, and leather. Easy to install and maintain.	Subfloor must be free of any defects or irregularities, which will telegraph through the surface of the tile.
Parquet	Instills the warm appearance of wood in a space. Available in a wide variety of sizes, colors, and patterns. Easy to install.	Damaged by water. Can scratch with friction from foot traffic and dirt. Color will deepen over time.
Leather	Soft, smooth, warm, and quiet underfoot. Comes in a wide variety of sizes, colors, shapes, and patterns. Easy to install and maintain.	Not for use in high-traffic or wet areas. Subfloor must be smooth or irregularities will show through the surface. Expensive.
Linoleum	All-natural material that is antistatic, antiallergenic, and antibiotic. It is warm, soft, and quiet underfoot. Environmentally friendly. Comes in a wide range of colors. Easy to install and maintain. Becomes stronger over the years. Affordable.	Not for use in wet areas. Subfloor must be smooth or irregularities will show through the surface.
Glass	Waterproof, stain-proof, and frost-proof. Available in an enormous varieties of size, shape, color, pattern, and texture. Blends well with other materials such as stone, ceramic, metal, and concrete. Easy to maintain.	Clear types difficult to install. Can scratch. Some types can be expensive.
Metal	Solid metal tiles are waterproof, stain-proof, and frost-proof. Made from virtually every type of metal, from aluminum to zinc. Numerous sizes, shapes, textures, and finishes available in addition to accents, trims, and borders. Blends wonderfully with stone, glass, concrete, and ceramic. Easy to install and care for.	Metal-coated tiles can scratch. Solid metal tiles will acquire a patina over the years; they can be brought back to a like-new appearance with metal cleaner if desired, though. Can be pricey in mass.

appendix: tables & charts

MATERIAL	PROS	CONS
Concrete	Available in a wide range of colors, sizes, shapes, textures, and finishes. Can resemble marble, aged stone, or suede, depending on the finish. Blends well with glass, metal, and other decorative materials.	Can stain and etch. Should be sealed with a penetrating sealer routinely. Cold and hard underfoot, but radiant heating and area rugs can alleviate these issues. Requires a strong subfloor.
Rubber	Soft, warm, and quiet underfoot. Available in a wide range of colors and surface textures. Very long-lasting, durable, and easy to care for.	Subfloor must be flat and smooth, or irregularities will telegraph through the surface. Some types can stain with grease and oil, and may need to be sealed. Rubber without a surface texture can be slippery when wet. Pricey.
Vinyl	Soft, warm and quiet underfoot. Comes in a wide range of colors, textures and finishes. Peel and stick varieties are very easy to install. Easy to care for. Damaged tiles easily removed and replaced. Inexpensive.	Subfloor must be flat and smooth, or irregularities will telegraph through the surface. Vinyl is a synthetic material that can off-gas. Flammable. Can dent, tear, and scuff. Less expensive types are not long-lasting. Can yellow with exposure to direct sunlight.

Metric Conversion Chart

Inches to millimeters to centimeters	Inches to centimeters to meters	Feet to meters
1 in. = 25.4 mm = 2.54 cm	1 in. = 2.54 cm = 0.025 m	1 ft = 0.305 m
1/16 in. = 1.59 mm = 0.16 cm	2 in. = 5.08 cm = 0.051 m	5 ft = 1.524 m
1/8 in. = 3.18 mm = 0.32cm	3 in. = 7.64 cm = 0.076 m	10 ft = 3.048 m
1/4 in. = 6.35 mm = 0.64 cm	4 in. = 10.16 cm = 0.102 m	25 ft = 7.62 m
3/8 in. = 9.53 mm = 0.95 cm	5 in. = 12.70 cm = 1.127 m	50 ft = 15.24 m
1/2 in. = 12.7 mm = 1.27 cm	6 in. = 15.24 cm = 0.152 m	
5/8 in. = 15.88 mm = 1.59 cm	7 in. = 17.78 cm = 0.178 m	
3/4 in. = 19.05 mm = 1.91 cm	8 in. = 20.32 cm = 0.203 m	
7/8 in. = 22.23 mm = 2.22 cm	9 in. = 22.86 cm = 0.229 m	
	10 in. = 25.40 cm = 0.254 m	
	11 in. = 27.94 cm = 0.279 m	
	12 in. = 30.48 cm = 0.305 m	

Coloring Books: Use these line drawings to spark your imagination (*courtesy Sonoma Tile Makers*).

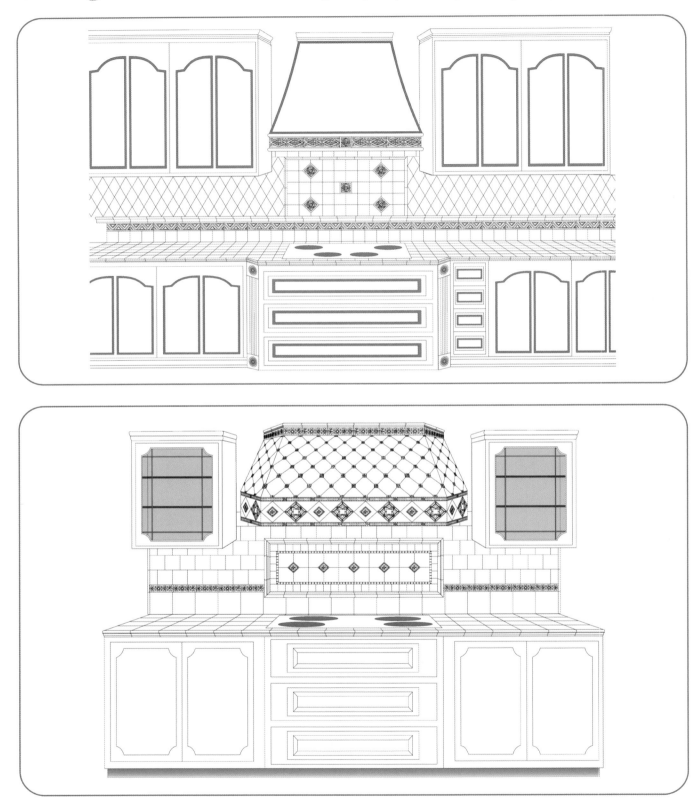

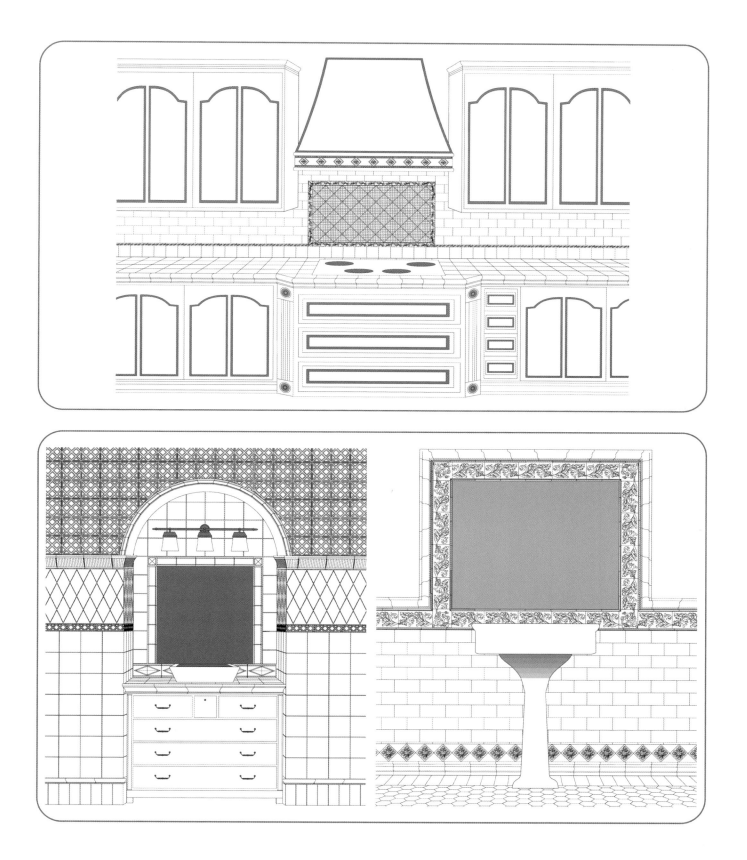

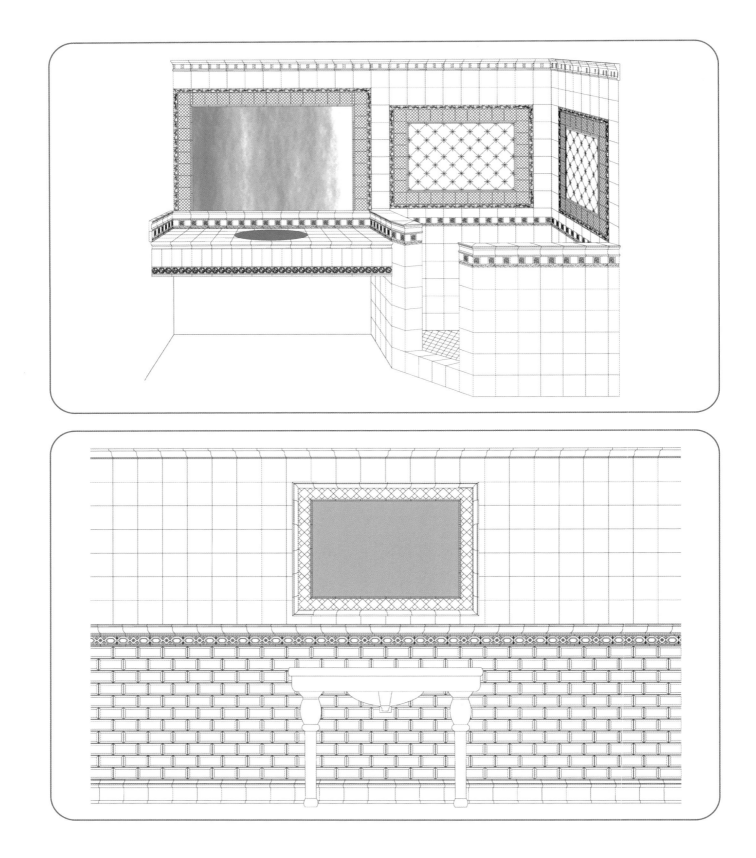

appendix: coloring books

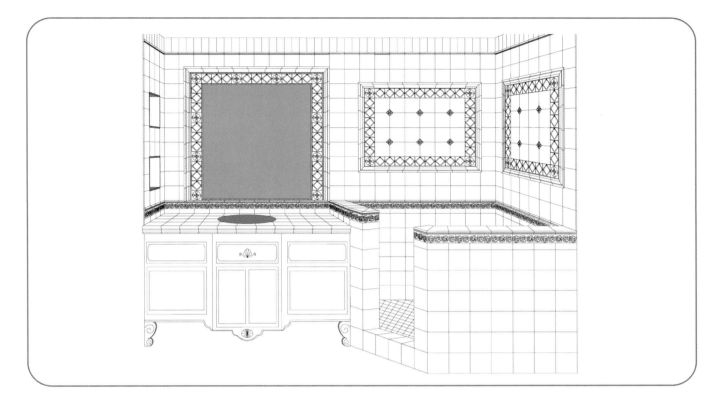

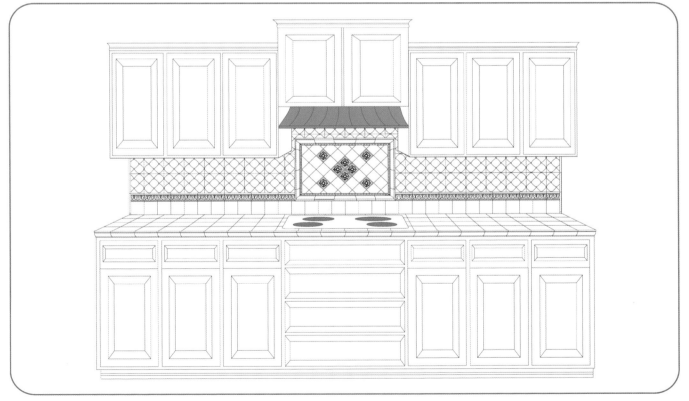

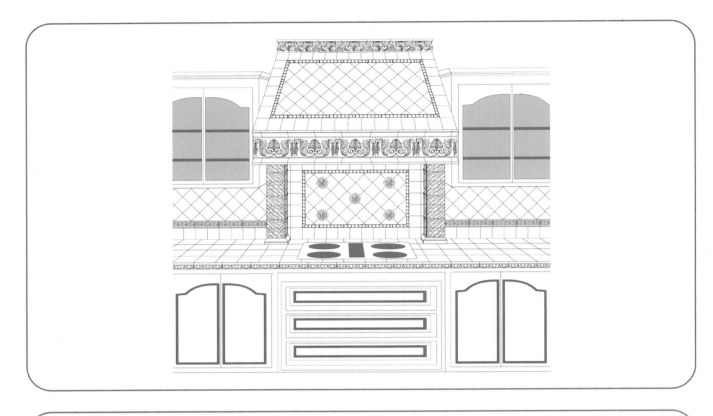

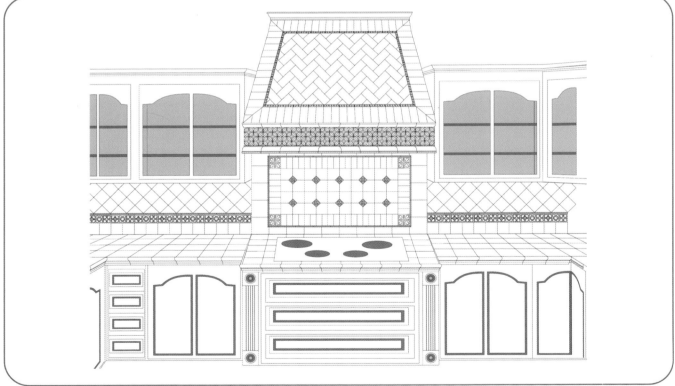

appendix: coloring books

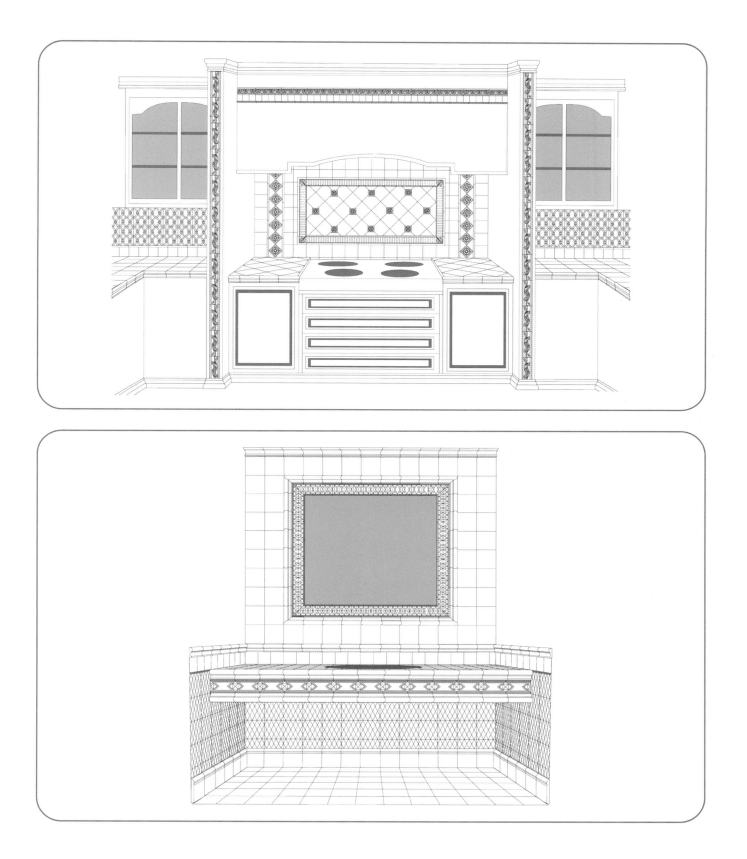

Tile Patterns

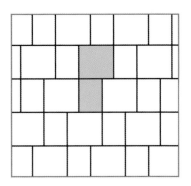 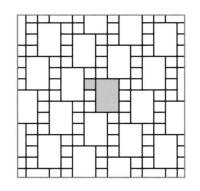 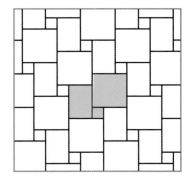

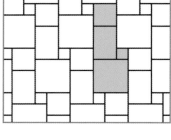 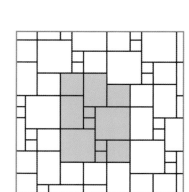 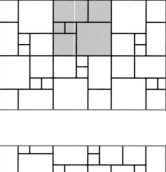 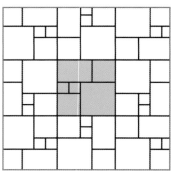 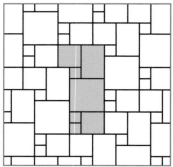

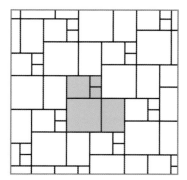 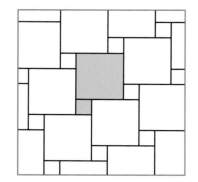 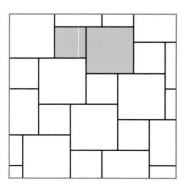

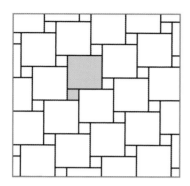
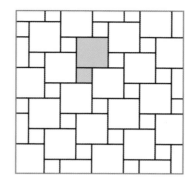
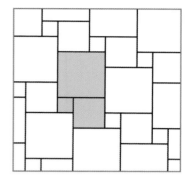

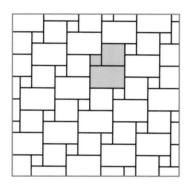

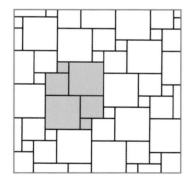
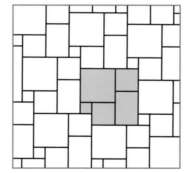

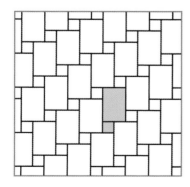
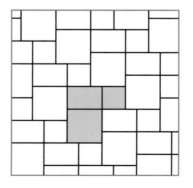

Tile Patterns

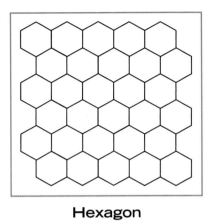

Hexagon

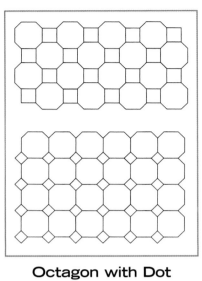

Octagon with Dot

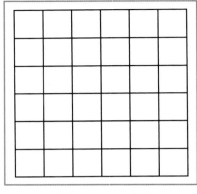

Square grid

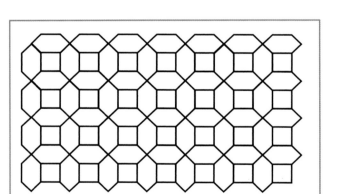

Lattice

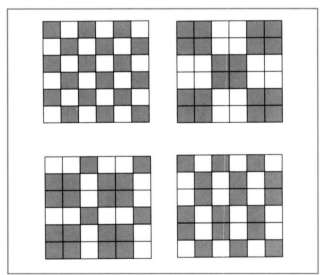

Checkerboard

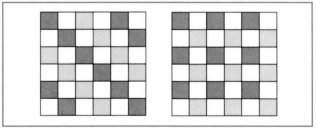

Quilted or Gingham

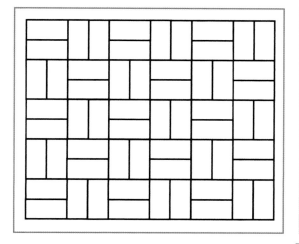

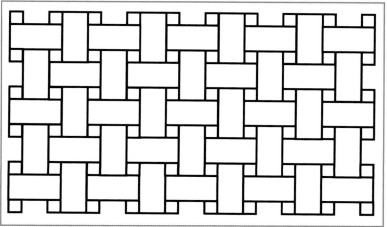

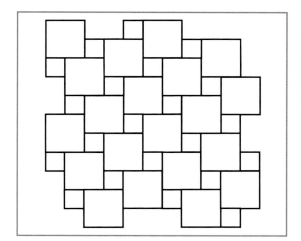

Basketweave

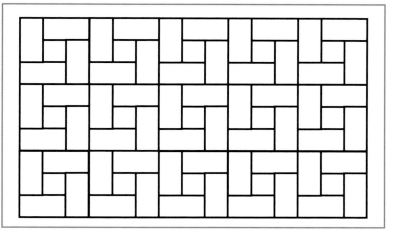

Pinwheel

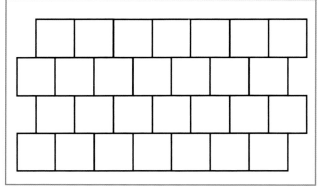

Offset

Running Board

Index

Index

Our home is often one of our biggest monetary investments, and it's where we spend the vast majority of our lives—so why not make it our castle? Give yourself permission to splurge on the focal points of your home, and never let anyone talk you out of your dreams. Tile can last a lifetime. Slow down, consider all of your options, and above all else . . . get what you love!